A LITTLE HISTORY OF RELIGION

Also by Richard Holloway

RICHARD HOLLOWAY

A LITTLE
HISTORY
of
RELIGION

YALE UNIVERSITY PRESS
NEW HAVEN AND LONDON

For information about this and other Yale University Press publications, please contact:
U.S. Office: sales.press@yale.edu   yalebooks.com
Europe Office: sales@yaleup.co.uk   yalebooks.co.uk

Set in Minion Pro by IDSUK (DataConnection) Ltd
Printed in the United States of America.

Library of Congress Cataloging-in-Publication Data

Names: Holloway, Richard, 1933- author.
Title: A little history of religion / Richard Holloway.
Description: New Haven : Yale University Press, [2016]
LCCN 2016013232 | ISBN 9780300208832 (cl : alk. paper)
LCSH: Religions. | Religion—History.
Classification: LCC BL80.3 .H65 2016 | DDC 200.9—dc23
LC record available at http://lccn.loc.gov/2016013232

A catalogue record for this book is available from the British Library.

ISBN 978-0-300-22881-6 (pbk)

10 9 8 7 6

Nick and Alice
With love

Contents

CHAPTER 1

Is Anybody There?

What is religion? And where does it come from? Religion comes from the mind of the human animal, so it comes from us. The other animals on earth don't seem to need a religion. And as far as we can tell they haven't developed any. That's because they are more at one with their lives than we are. They act instinctively. They go with the flow of existence without thinking about it all the time. The human animal has lost the ability to do that. Our brains have developed in a way that makes us self-conscious. We are interested in ourselves. We can't help wondering about things. We can't help *thinking*.

And the biggest thing we think about is the universe itself and where it came from. Is there somebody out there who made it? The shorthand word we use for this possible somebody or something is *God, theos* in Greek. Someone who thinks there is a god out there is called a *theist*. Someone who thinks there's nobody out there and we're on our own in the universe is called an *atheist*. And the study of the god and what it wants from us is called *theology*. The other big question we can't help asking ourselves is what happens to us after death. When we die, is that it or is there anything else to come? If there is something else, what will it be like?

What we call religion was our first crack at answering these questions. Its answer to the first question was simple. The universe was created by a power beyond itself that some call God, that continues to be interested and involved in what it has created. The individual religions all offer different versions of what the power called God is like and what it wants from us, but they all believe in its existence in some form or other. They tell us we are not alone in the universe. Beyond us there are other realities, other dimensions. We call them 'supernatural' because they are outside the natural world, the world immediately available to our senses.

If religion's most important belief is the existence of a reality beyond this world that we call God, what prompted the belief and when did it start? It began ages ago. In fact, there doesn't seem to have been a time when human beings didn't believe in the existence of a supernatural world beyond this one. And wondering about what happened to people after they died may have been what started it off. All animals die, but unlike the others, humans don't leave their dead to decompose where they drop. As far back as we can follow their traces, humans seem to have given their dead funerals. And how they planned them tells us something about their earliest beliefs.

Of course, this is not to say that other animals don't mourn their dead companions. There is plenty of evidence that many of them do. In Edinburgh there is a famous statue of a little dog called Greyfriars Bobby that testifies to the grief animals feel when they lose someone they are attached to. Bobby died in 1872 after spending the last fourteen years of his life lying on the grave of his dead master, John Gray. There is no doubt that Bobby missed his friend, but it was John Gray's human family who gave him a proper funeral and laid him to rest in Greyfriars Kirkyard. And in burying him they performed one of the most distinctive human acts. So what prompted humans to start burying their dead?

The most obvious thing we notice about the dead is that something that used to happen in them has stopped happening.

They no longer breathe. It was a small step to associate the act of breathing with the idea of something dwelling within yet separate from the physical body that gave it life. The Greek word for it was *psyche*, the Latin *spiritus*, both from verbs meaning to breathe or blow. A spirit or soul was what made a body live and breathe. It inhabited the body for a time. And when the body died it departed. But where did it go? One explanation was that it went back to the world beyond, the spirit world, the flipside of the one we inhabit on earth.

What we discover of early funeral rites supports that view, though all our distant forebears left us are silent traces of what they might have been thinking. Writing hadn't been invented, so they couldn't leave their thoughts or describe their beliefs in a form we can read today. But they did leave us clues about what they were thinking. So let's start examining them. To find them we have to go back thousands of years BCE, a term that needs an explanation before we move on.

It makes sense to have a global calendar or way of dating when things happened in the past. The one we use now was devised by Christianity in the sixth century CE, showing just how influential religion has been in our history. For thousands of years the Catholic Church was one of the great powers on earth, so powerful it even fixed the calendar the world still uses. The pivotal event was the birth of its founder, Jesus Christ. His birth was Year One. Anything that happened before it was BC or Before Christ. Anything that came after it was AD or *anno Domini*, the year of the Lord.

In our time BC and AD were replaced by BCE and CE, terms that can be translated with or without a religious twist: either Before the Christian Era for BCE and within the Christian Era for CE, or Before the Common Era for BCE or within the Common Era for CE. You can take your pick as to how you understand the terms. In this book I'll use BCE to locate events that happened Before Christ or Before the Common Era. But to avoid cluttering the text I'll be more sparing in my use of CE and will only use it when I think it's necessary. So if you come across a date on its own you'll know it happened within the Christian or Common Era.

Anyway, we find evidence from about 130000 BCE onwards of some kind of religious belief in the way our ancestors buried their dead. Food, tools and ornaments were placed in the graves that have been discovered, suggesting a belief that the dead travelled on to some kind of afterlife and needed to be equipped for the journey. Another practice was the painting of the bodies of the dead with red ochre, maybe to symbolise the idea of continuing life. This was discovered in one of the oldest known burials, of a mother and child at Qafzeh in Israel in 100000 BCE. And the same practice is found half a world away, at Lake Mungo in Australia in 42000 BCE, where the body was also covered in red ochre. Painting the dead marks the emergence of one of humanity's cleverest ideas, symbolic thinking. There's lot of it in religion, so it's worth getting hold of it.

As with many useful words, *symbol* comes from Greek. It means to bring together things that had come apart, the way you might glue the bits of a broken plate together. Then a symbol became an object that stood for or represented something else. It still had the idea of joining things up, but it had become more complicated than simply glueing bits of pottery together. A good example of a symbol is a national flag, such as the Stars and Stripes. When we see the Stars and Stripes it brings the USA to mind. It *symbolises* it, stands in for it.

Symbols become sacred to people because they represent loyalties deeper than words can express. That's why they hate to see their symbols violated. There is nothing wrong with burning a piece of old cloth, but if it happens to symbolise your nation it might make you angry. When the symbols are religious, sacred to a particular community, they become even more potent. And insulting them can provoke murderous fury. Hold the idea of symbol in your mind because it will come up again and again in this book. The thought is that one thing, such as red ochre, stands for another thing, such as the belief that the dead go on to a new life in another place.

Another example of symbolic thinking was the way in which marking where the dead lay became important, especially if they were powerful and significant figures. Sometimes they were laid under gigantic boulders, sometimes in carefully constructed stone chambers called dolmens, which consisted of two upright stones supporting a large lid. The most dramatic of humanity's monuments to the dead are the pyramids at Giza in Egypt. As well as being tombs, the pyramids might be thought of as launch pads from which the souls of their royal occupants had been blasted into immortality.

In time burial rites became not only more elaborate, but in some places they became frighteningly cruel, with the sacrifice of wives and servants who were sent along to maintain the comfort and status of the deceased in their life on the other side. It is worth noting that from the beginning there was a ruthless side to religion that had little regard for the lives of individuals.

A good reading of these clues is that our forebears saw death as the entrance to another phase of existence, imagined as a version of this one. And we catch a glimpse of their belief in a world beyond this one, yet connected to it, with death as the door between them.

So far religious beliefs look as if they might have been acquired by a process of inspired guess work. Our ancestors asked themselves where the world came from and figured it must have been created by a higher power somewhere out there. They looked at the unbreathing dead and decided their spirits must have left the bodies they once inhabited and gone somewhere else.

But an important group in the history of religion don't *guess* the existence of the world beyond or the destination of departed souls. They tell us they have visited it or been visited by it. They have heard the demands it makes of us. They have been commanded to tell others what they have seen and heard. So they proclaim the message they have received. They attract followers who believe their words and start living according to their teaching. We call them prophets or sages. And it is through them that new religions are born.

Then something else happens. The story they tell is memorised by their followers. At first it is passed on by word of mouth. But in time it is written down in words on paper. It then becomes what we call Holy Scripture or sacred writing. The *Bible!* *The* Book! And it becomes the religion's most potent symbol. It is a physical book, obviously. It was written by men. We can trace its history. But through its words a message from the world beyond is brought into our world. The book becomes a bridge that links eternity with time. It connects the human with the divine. That is why it is looked upon with awe and studied with intensity. And it is why believers hate it when it is derided or destroyed.

The history of religion is the story of these prophets and sages and the movements they started and the scriptures that were written about them. But it is a subject that is heavy with controversy and disagreement. Sceptics wonder whether some of these prophets even existed. And they doubt the claims made in their visions and voices. Fair enough, but that is to miss the point. What is beyond dispute is that they exist in the *stories* told about them, stories that still carry meaning for billions of people today.

In this book we'll read the stories the religions tell us about themselves without constantly asking whether that was the way things actually happened back then. But because it would be wrong to ignore that question entirely, we'll spend the next chapter thinking about what was going on when those prophets and sages saw visions and heard voices. One of those prophets was called Moses.

CHAPTER 2

The Doors

Say you found yourself in the Sinai desert in Egypt one morning in 1300 BCE. You might come across a bearded barefoot man kneeling before a thorn bush. You watch him as he listens intently to the bush. Then he speaks to it. He listens again. Finally he gets to his feet and strides away with a purposeful air. The man's name is Moses, one of the most famous prophets in the history of religion and founder of the Jewish religion. The story that will one day be written about him will say that on this day a god spoke to him from a burning bush and commanded him to lead a band of slaves out of Egypt into freedom in the Promised Land of Palestine.

To you, the observer, the bush is not burning with a fire that does not consume itself. It is ablaze with red berries. And while you notice how attentive Moses is as he listens, you can't hear what is being said to him though you can make out his replies. But you are not particularly surprised by any of this. Your little sister has animated conversations with her dolls. And you have a young cousin who talks to an imaginary friend who is as real to him as his own parents. You may also have heard mentally ill people having intense conversations with unseen listeners. So you are used to the idea that there are people who hear voices no one else can pick up.

But let's turn from Moses for the moment and think about the unseen speaker who is addressing him. Fix in your mind the idea of an invisible reality outside time and space that can communicate directly with human beings. Get hold of that thought and you will have grasped the central idea of religion. There is a power in the universe beyond what is available to our physical senses *and it has made itself known to special people who proclaim its message to others.* For the moment we are neither agreeing nor disagreeing with that statement. We are just trying to pin it down. *There is an invisible force out there that we call God and it has been in touch!* That's the claim. As we pursue this history we'll learn that the different religions all have different versions of this claim and what it has been trying to tell us. But most of them take for granted that it's there. And that their form of belief is the best response to its existence.

Now let's go back to Moses and think about his side of that encounter in the desert. To you the bush wasn't on fire nor could you hear the god's voice booming out of it. So how come Moses felt the heat of the flames and listened so intently to what the voice commanded him to do and did it? Was it only happening inside his head, which is why you couldn't see what was going on? Or could his mind have been in touch with another mind that was beyond your reach and understanding? If religions start with experiences in the minds of their prophets and sages, and if you want to give them a fair hearing and not just dismiss them as fantasy, then you are going to have to consider whether some people may be open to realities the rest of us are blind and deaf to.

A possible explanation is that our minds operate on two different levels, like a ground-floor apartment with a basement or cellar underneath. We experience the difference when we dream. During the day the conscious mind is awake on the ground floor, living its planned and ordered life. But when it puts out the light and goes to sleep at night the door from the cellar opens and fills our dreaming mind with jumbled fragments of unspoken desires and forgotten fears. So if we can set aside for the moment the question of whether there is more to the universe than meets the eye, we can at least acknowledge that there is more to *us* than our regular, waking conscious lives. There is an underground basement in the human mind called the subconscious and when we sleep its door opens and through it flood the images and voices we call dreaming.

In the history of religion we will find people who in their waking hours have the kind of encounters the rest of us have only in dreams. We call them prophet and dreamers, but another way to think of them might be as creative artists who, rather than pouring their visions into paintings or novels, are impelled to translate them into messages that persuade millions to believe in what they have seen and heard. And Moses is a famous example of this mysterious activity. Something got in touch with him from somewhere and because of that meeting the history of the Jewish people changed forever. But what was the something and where did it come from? Was it inside him? Was it outside him? Or could it have been both at the same time?

Taking what happened to Moses in Sinai as an example and using the metaphor of the door between our conscious and subconscious minds to help us, let me suggest an approach that offers three different ways of thinking about religious experience.

In an event of this kind the door between the subconscious and the conscious mind opens. What follows is like a dream. Prophets believe it is coming from outside them, but it is actually coming from their own subconscious. The voice they hear is real. It speaks to them. But it is their own voice, coming from inside their own mind. That's why no one else can hear it.

Or it could be that two doors are open in a prophetic experience. The subconscious or dreaming mind may have access to the supernatural world beyond. If there is another reality out there, or a mind beyond our minds, it is not unlikely that it would try to get in touch with us. What happens to prophets in a revelation is that they encounter that other reality and its mind speaks to their mind. And they tell the world what it has told them.

There's a middle position between the One Door theory and the Two Door theory. Yes, there may be two doors in the human subconscious. And the human mind may have genuine encounters with what's out there. But we know how unreliable humans are at understanding other human minds, so we should be wary about the claims they make about their encounters with the divine mind. There may well be two doors in the human subconscious mind, but the one that opens onto the other world is unlikely ever to be completely ajar, so we can't be certain about what the prophets claim to have seen and heard.

Let us use my doors metaphor to look again at what happened to Moses in the desert and the three different approaches to religion it suggests. If you take the One Door approach, Moses had a dream that gave him the strength and resolution to become the liberator of his people from slavery in Egypt, a story we'll look at more closely in a later chapter. The experience was genuine. It happened. But it came entirely from his subconscious mind. A good analogy for this approach to religion comes from the old movie theatres I loved as a boy. In those days films were imprinted onto reels of celluloid. At the back of the cinema above the balcony there was a booth from which the pictures were projected onto the silver screen on the opposite wall. What we saw from where we sat was in front of us, but it actually came from the machine behind us. One way to think about religion is as a projection of the fears and longings of our subconscious mind onto the screen of life. Religion seems to be out there and to have a life of its own. But it actually comes from the depths of our own imagination. It's an entirely human production.

You can stop there and leave it at that or you can accept most of that description *and* step through the idea of the Second Door. Without changing a detail of the human side of religious experience, it is possible to believe that it came from God as well. We couldn't hear the voice Moses was listening to because it was a case of the mind of the god communicating directly to the mind of Moses. Invisible and inaudible to us, it was a real encounter with another reality. We can't fully comprehend the event, but we do see its results.

And a further turn can be given to the idea of the Second Door. Knowing how easy it is for human beings to misunderstand everyday encounters with other humans, they should be wary about the claims they make for their encounters with God, and treat them with scepticism and modesty. This means we should apply our critical faculties to religious claims and not just take them at their own self-evaluation.

So you can be a non-believer, a true believer or a critical believer. As you think about these matters you may even find yourself switching from position to position over the years, as many do. I'll leave you to make up your own mind about the best way to interpret the stories you'll read in this book. Or to leave the matter undecided until the last page. And you may even decide not to decide, a position known as *agnosticism*, from a Greek word meaning 'unknowable'.

So far we have been thinking about religion in general terms. Now it's time to look at the individual religions in particular. But where to start is an interesting question, as is what order we should follow. Unlike the history of science or philosophy, taking a strictly chronological approach to religion won't work. Different things were going on in different places at the same time, so we can't just follow a continuous line of development. We'll have to zigzag both chronologically and geographically.

The advantage of that approach is that it will show us how varied were the answers the different religions gave to the big questions humanity has been asking itself since the beginning. The questions may have been the same – 'Is there anybody out there? And what happens to us after death?' – but the answers have been very different. That's what makes the history of religion so fascinating.

Thankfully there seems to be an obvious starting point for our journey. It has to be with the oldest and in many ways the most complicated of the living religions, Hinduism. So we'll begin with India.

CHAPTER 3

The Wheel

A popular theme in science fiction is the hero who goes back in time to alter events in the past that had a catastrophic effect on human history. At the beginning of one story a train is hurtling along the tracks with a mad bomber on board. He blows the train up as it passes a huge dam, causing a flood of water to drown a whole city. Fortunately, a secret government department has perfected a way of sending people back in time. Using its new device, it gets an agent onto the train before it leaves the station, giving him two hours to find the bomber and disable the bomb. He succeeds just in time and the city is saved. Most of us have wished we could go back in time like that to delete a message or restrain an impulse that hurt others and brought us unhappiness. But the law of consequences (or one thing follows another) takes over and we are stuck with the result of what we did.

In Hindu religion this is called *karma* or the law of the deed. But its scope is not just the life you are living now. According to Hindu teaching, your soul or spirit has had many lives in the past before you came into the one you are going through at the moment. And you will live many more lives in the future when this one is over. Each of these lives is determined by how you acted in the one before and the one before that and the one before that, away back into the mists of antiquity. Just as how you are behaving now will influence the kind of life you'll get on the next turn of the wheel.

When the prophets and sages of India looked into the distance and wondered what happened to human beings when they died, they received a remarkable answer. People did not die, either in the sense that they ceased to exist altogether or in the sense that they went on as they were into some other kind of life beyond death. No, they came back to earth again in another life form dictated by their karma. And it might not be as a human being. The whole of existence was a great recycling factory in which the quality of the life that went through the door marked Death affected the status of what emerged through the door on the other side marked Rebirth. The name of the factory was _samsāra_ (meaning wandering through), because souls were carried through it to their next shape and the next. For good or ill, every action they committed in one life affected the quality of their next appearance. And it was not just the human creature that was trapped in samsāra. The world itself was subject to the same law of death and rebirth. At the end of its current cycle of existence it would fall into a state of repose, from which it would be called back into being when the time was ripe. So the wheel of existence turned and turned and turned again.

But they did not think of karma as a punishment devised by some supernatural inspector of souls. Karma was an impersonal law like gravity, in which one thing came from another as effect followed cause, like tapping one domino and watching all the others fall. In its wanderings through samsāra the soul might get through as many as eight million appearances before it finally achieved _moksha_, or release from existence, and lost itself in eternity like a raindrop falling into the ocean. And how to escape from the endless turning of the wheel of existence and achieve salvation was the ultimate purpose of Hindu religion.

The technical term for this description of what happens to us after death is _reincarnation_. It has been believed in by many communities throughout the world, but nowhere with the intensity achieved in Indian religion. All the terms I used to define it – *karma*, the law of the deed, *samsāra*, the wandering of the soul in search of *moksha* or release – come from an ancient language called Sanskrit. It was brought into India by a band of wild invaders from the north. And it is with their eruption into India around 2000 BCE that we can date the beginnings of Hinduism.

In the faraway north above India there was a long stretch of grassland called the Central Asian Steppes. It was rough prairie country, ideal for the kind of hard-riding cowboys who followed their grazing cattle in constant search for the best pasture. For reasons we are not quite sure of, around the beginning of the second millennium BCE these people began to migrate from the steppes in search of a better life. Many of them rode south into India. They called themselves compatriots, or *Aryans* in their own language. They were a warlike people who drove fast chariots. And they swept in waves into the Indus Valley in the north-west corner of the subcontinent.

A sophisticated civilisation already existed there. It had advanced systems of art, architecture and religion. And it would have possessed the vices as well as the virtues of all developed societies. It was into this scene that those Aryan invaders galloped, and they made up in energy and courage for what they lacked in refinement. Another factor that distinguished the invaders from the natives was that their skins were lighter, and into that difference in skin colour much would be read that would echo down the centuries to our own time, giving an ugly ring to the very word Aryan. But the raiders brought more than their light skins into India. They also brought their gods with them and the beginnings of a remarkable body of religious literature called *Vedas*.

In their written form, the Vedas were composed between 1200 and 1000 BCE as the Aryans entrenched themselves in India and dominated its life. Known as *Shruti*, or 'hearing', the Vedas were understood in two distinct but related senses. Their substance had been heard originally by the sages of the past who had waited for the meaning of existence to be disclosed to them from beyond.

They were the original hearers, the ones to whom the voices had spoken. And what they had heard was listened to again and again by their disciples as it was repeated to them by their teachers. In this way the content of the Vedas was passed on down the centuries. Reading them aloud is still the preferred method of learning the Hindu scriptures. You won't find a 'Bible' or a 'Qur'an' in a Hindu temple, but you will hear its spoken equivalent in the ceremonies that are practised there.

Veda means 'knowledge'. The word has the same root as the English words 'wit' and 'wisdom'. There are four Vedas – the *Rig Veda*, the *Yajur Veda*, the *Sama Veda* and the *Atharva Veda*, each of them with four parts. They are divided into the *Samhitas*, the *Brahmanas*, the *Aranyahas* and the *Upanishads*. Here's a quick word about them. The Rig Veda Samhita is the oldest of the four Vedas. It contains over a thousand hymns praising the gods. In religion this activity is called 'worship', and one way to think of it is as the kind of flattery powerful rulers are supposed to enjoy, much in the way the British Queen is addressed as 'Your Majesty' and people are expected to bow or curtsy when they meet her. Here's an example from the Rig Veda:

This worshiping of gods makes me sick, as it would any admirable god,

> Maker of All, exceeding wise, exceeding strong,
> Creator, Ordainer, highest Exemplar . . .

You get the idea. Lay it on thick! And just as earthly monarchs enjoy receiving gifts as well as being smothered in compliments, so it was with the gods. If hymns are the flattery we offer the gods, then sacrifices are the gifts that accompany them. And they have to be presented in careful ceremonies that require skilled professionals to conduct them. In the Hindu tradition the priests who conducted the sacrifices were called *Brahmins* and the instruction manuals they compiled to help them were called *Brahmanas*.

Directories of this sort are boring to most people, but they can be obsessively interesting to a certain kind of religious mind. When I was a young man studying to be a priest I was fascinated by guides to the rites and ceremonies of the different Christian traditions.

There was a tome the size of a doorstep called *The Ceremonies of the Roman Rite Described*, as well as a pale Church of England version called *Ritual Notes*. I used to dip excitedly into both to picture regiments of bishops processing slowly into vast cathedrals smothered in the smoke of sweet incense. Those books were the Brahmanas of Catholic Christianity. But it is not only religious officials who love dressing up and performing elaborate rituals. Many private clubs and student fraternities have their own secret traditions, reminders of the human need for symbolism and ceremony.

symbols of the group, of the tribe.

If, like me, you are more interested in a religion's inner beliefs than in its external rituals, then the final stage of Vedic evolution is the one that should engage your attention. It comes in the *Upanishads*, written over a period of about three centuries and completed around 300 BCE. The Upanishads – or 'sittings near a teacher' – move the interest away from the performance or ceremonial side of Hinduism to its philosophical and theological aspects. It is in the Upanishads that we first come across the doctrine of karma and samsāra that we explored at the beginning of this chapter.

In the next chapter we'll explore the emergence of some of these distinctive Hindu teachings and the way they were explained. But I want to end this chapter by turning to the Hindu response to religion's other big question. We have already seen how they answered the question about what happened to us after death. The answer of the Upanishads was the remarkable doctrine of reincarnation. The other question religion always asks is what, if anything, is out there in the darkness beyond the universe. The other religions usually name the prophets who gave them the answers to these questions and whose name they take as their own. That's not how it went in Hinduism. There was no founder from whom the religion takes its name, no single figure it looked back to as its inspiration. It came from unnamed dreamers in India's deep past. But while it may not have kept the names of those early dreamers, it kept what they told them.

And in the Rig Veda it begins to answer religion's question about what's out there. To hear it we have to imagine ourselves beside a camp fire under the star-studded North Indian sky as one of their unknown sages pierces through time to the beginning of the world and beyond. He is chanting rather than speaking as he gazes raptly into the night.

> Then was not non-existent nor existent: there
>   was no realm of air, no sky beyond it.
> That One Thing, without breath, breathed by its own nature:
>   apart from it was nothing whatsoever.
> The gods are later than this world's production. Who knows,
>   then, whence it first came into being?
> He, the first of this creation, whether he formed it all
>   or did not form it.
> Whose eye controls this world in highest heaven, he verily
>   knows it, or perhaps he knows it not.

There are surprises in what we hear him chanting. There are 'gods', we are told, but they 'are later than this world's production'. That means that they, like us, were *made* and are also subject to the revolutions of the wheel of time. They come and go like the rest of us. But the dreamer hints that behind all the shape-shifting there is something that does not change, 'that One Thing' he calls it. It's as if history and its creatures were like mists that cloak and distort the presence of a great mountain: that One Thing! But what is it? And who are the gods who are its agents?

CHAPTER 4

One Into Many

One day you hear that your favourite author is coming to town to talk about her work. You go along to the bookshop where she is appearing and hear her reading from the new book, which is filled with the latest adventures of characters long familiar to you. You ask her where they all come from. Are they real? Do they exist somewhere? She laughs. 'Only in my imagination', she says. She made them all up. They come from her head. So she can do anything she likes with them.

What if it hits you on the way home that you might not be real either? That you might be someone else's creation, a character in a plot dreamed up by someone else? Were that to happen it would be as if a character in a book came to realise that he or she had no independent life and was simply the product of some writer's imagination.

That was like the idea that hit the sages of India with the force of a revelation. They themselves were not real! Only one thing was ultimately real: the Universal Soul or Spirit they called *Brahman*, which expressed or wrote itself in many forms. Everything in the world that appeared to exist in hard reality was, in fact, an aspect of Brahman in its many disguises and shapes. It was, as the Upanishads say, 'hidden in all beings . . . the self within all beings, watching over all works, dwelling in all beings, the witness, the perceiver, the only one'. And they were in Brahman and Brahman was in them!

A story from the Upanishads captures the closeness of this identity in a famous phrase. A father said to his son, 'That which is the finest essence – this whole world has that as its soul. That is Reality . . . And . . . That art thou, Shvetaketu'. People may think they have a separate, individual existence, but that is an illusion. They are all characters who appear again and again in Brahman's unfolding storyline, their roles in the next episode scripted by their karma.

And it was not only individuals whose roles had been written for them. The way society had been organised into different classes or castes had also been scripted. Every time a human soul was reborn, it found itself in one of these groups and had to live out its time there until its next death and reincarnation. Since there was a clear link between the separate castes and their colour, we should remember that the Aryan invaders who brought their language and religion into the Indus Valley were light-skinned and probably looked down on the darker skinned races they encountered when they arrived. Some sort of division into different castes may have existed in India before the Aryans, but they justified it as an arrangement ordered by the Supreme Reality. And there was a scripture that described its origin.

Brahman had delegated the task of making this world to a creator god confusingly called *Brahma*. Brahma made the first man, *Manu*, and the first woman, *Shatarupa*. And from them came forth humanity. But human beings were not created equal. There were four castes in descending order of importance. At the top were the *Brahmins*, the priests and teachers. Next came the *Kshatriyas*, the kings, aristocrats and warriors. After them came the *Vaisyas*, the traders, merchants and craftsmen. And at the bottom came the *Sudra*, the servants and farm labourers. Brahmins were fair. Kshatriyas were reddish. Vaisyas were yellowish. Sudras were black. And beneath them all was a class whose work, such as emptying latrines and other dirty work, rendered them permanently unclean. They were the 'untouchables' whose very shadow polluted what it fell across. It was a hard and rigid system, but belief in karma and samsāra took some of the despair out of it. Wandering through the lives karma determined for them, people could always hope that by living well they might improve their position next time round.

But the world with its castes and divisions and teeming forms of life was not the only way in which Brahman expressed himself. He created gods as well, millions of them. They were yet another way in which the One Without Shape assumed different shapes. But we have to be careful about how we think of these gods. On the surface Hinduism is what we call *polytheistic*. That's another way of saying it believes in many gods. But it could just as accurately be described as *monotheistic*, because its many gods are all believed to be aspects or expressions of the one God. But even the idea of 'one God' isn't quite right. In Hindu belief, behind all the shifting illusory characters who flit through life – including the 'gods' – there is one Supreme Reality, 'that One Thing', as the Upanishads expressed it. If you like to learn the technical terms for things, this belief is known as *monism*, meaning 'one-thing-ism' rather than 'one-god-ism'.

Since not everyone has the kind of mind that is comfortable with an idea as big as that, images of the gods as symbols of 'that One Thing' were made available to give people something to look at and concentrate on. Remember: a symbol is an object that stands for and connects us to a big idea. In Hinduism there are thousands of gods and thousands of images to choose from, all designed to draw the thoughts of the worshipper to the One through whom everything that exists came to be.

If you want to see what Hindu gods are like the place to look for them is in one of their temples, so let's find the nearest one. We walk up the steps into a porch where we remove our shoes and enter the temple barefoot. We come to the central hall and at the far end, up more steps, we'll discover the shrine to the god or gods who live there. Large temples in India are teeming with gods. The one we've chosen houses only three but they are very popular and important.

Here's a statue of a dancing man with three eyes and four arms, from whose head flows India's most famous river, the Ganges. Here is a large human figure with a pot belly and the head of an elephant. But our most disconcerting discovery must be this painting of a woman with her tongue sticking out as far as it will go. She has four arms, in one of which she holds a sharp sword and in another a severed head from which blood drips.

The dancing figure with three eyes and four arms is Shiva the Destroyer. The elephant-headed god is Ganesh, one of Shiva's sons born to the goddess Parvati. And the four-armed woman holding the severed head is Kali, another of Shiva's wives. Ganesh has the head of an elephant because one day his father failed to recognise him and chopped his head off. On realising his mistake he promised him a transplant from the first creature he came across – which turned out to be an elephant. As befits one who has endured such an ordeal, Ganesh is a popular and approachable deity who helps his followers meet the challenges life throws at them.

Kali's story is less consoling. The gods of Hinduism are great shape-shifters, and Kali is one of the many forms of the mother goddess, the feminine aspect of God. In one of her battles against evil, Kali got so carried away with the thrill of destruction that she slaughtered everything in front of her. To stop her, Shiva threw himself at her feet. Kali was so shocked by his action that her tongue stuck out in surprise. Kali and Ganesh are colourful figures, but Shiva is more important. He is the most memorable of a triad of top gods in the Hindu pantheon, the other two being Brahma the Creator, whom we've already met, and Vishnu the Preserver.

To grasp the place of the three top gods in Hindu religion we have to understand two different ways of thinking about time. In Western thought time goes like an arrow fired at a target, so its best image is a straight line like this: ———➤ In Indian thought, time turns like a wheel, so its best image is a circle like this: ○ Just as their karma propels individuals through cycle after cycle of rebirth, so is the universe subject to a similar law. At the end of its present term it fades into the void of emptiness, until that One Thing starts the wheel of time spinning again and Brahma brings another universe into existence.

His duty done until the next turn of the wheel, Brahma relaxes and Vishnu takes over. Vishnu, usually depicted with a mace in his right hand as a symbol of authority, is the god who cherishes the world like a loving parent and works hard to keep it safe. Vishnu is comforting and reassuring, maybe even a bit boring. Shiva is far from boring. He represents the warlike side of human nature. He is the terminator who ends what Brahma started and Vishnu sustained. His most dramatic action is the Dance of Death when he tramples time and the world back into oblivion until the next turn of the wheel.

As devout Hindus gaze at the images of the gods and reflect on what they represent, they are reminded of the turning of the great wheel of time which spins them on and on into life after life. It is a revolving stage on which they all come and go, appearing and disappearing, making their entrances and their exits, a brilliant but wearying spectacle. Is there any way in which they can manage to quit the stage and retire? Is a final exit from the comings and goings of samsāra possible?

There are disciplines the soul can practise that will help it escape from the revolving stage of time, but to understand them we have to remember the predicament humans find themselves in. They themselves are not real, yet they are trapped in the illusion that they are. Salvation is to achieve release from that illusion and let the self finally disappear. For simplicity's sake we can divide the disciplines that bring release nearer into two different kinds of spiritual practice. We might think of them as the external way and the internal way; the way of concentrating on something and the way of concentrating on nothing.

In following the external way, also known as the way of loving devotion, worshippers use the shape or image of a god to achieve communion with the One Without Shape. They bring gifts to their god in the temple and tend him with loving care. In performing these rituals they are going out from themselves into the One. It promotes a kind of self-forgetfulness that gradually releases them from the clutches of the human nature that has trapped them in illusion. But it's slow work and may take countless lives before the final escape from the wheel of constant return is achieved.

The other path to salvation takes the opposite approach. It does not use images to reach what is beyond appearance. It tries to empty itself of the illusion of the self by the practice of meditation. By learning to sit still and ignore the discomfort of their bodies and the distractions that race through their minds, its practitioners try to empty themselves of the illusion of the self and achieve union with the Real. But meditation is not a quick fix either. The sense of union it brings is fleeting. And the empty mind soon fills up again with all its familiar cravings and distractions. That is why, in pursuit of a permanent state of self-forgetfulness and union with the One, some abandon all earthly attachments and become wandering beggars who live a life of complete self-denial. They suppress the needs of the body that bind them to this life in order to lose themselves in the One who alone is real.

Hinduism does hold out the promise of final liberation from the wheel of time, but the thought of the infinity of lives it may take to achieve salvation stuns the heart. Around 500 BCE it prompted some to wonder whether there might not be a quicker way to obtain that longed-for release. It is the answer given by one of the most attractive geniuses in the history of religion to which we must next turn. His name was Siddhartha Gautama and he was a prince. But he is better known as the Buddha.

CHAPTER 5

Prince to Buddha

Fifteen hundred years after those Aryan horsemen thundered into India and began the evolution of the complex and colourful religion we now call Hinduism, a man looked in dismay at its doctrine of endless reincarnations. He asked himself what it was that shackled souls onto the wheel of samsāra. And from his answer a new spiritual movement emerged. He was born around 580 BCE at the foot of the Himalayan Mountains in north-east India. His name was Siddhartha Gautama and this is his story.

Siddhartha belonged to the Kshatriya caste of rulers and warriors. His father, Suddhodhana, King of the Sakyas, was fifty years old when his wife Queen Maya gave birth to their son. A devout child, Siddhartha studied the Vedas, the sacred books of Hinduism. And though he was a prince who lived a privileged life, his teachers reminded him that, like everyone else, he was on a long journey through many lives. When he was sixteen he married Princess Yosodhara and they had a son Rahula. Until he was twenty-nine Siddhartha led a privileged and protected life, his every need met by an army of servants. But in the space of a few days a series of events changed his life for ever. It became known as the story of the Four Sights.

On the first day, coming back from a day's hunting, Siddhartha saw an emaciated man writhing in pain on the ground. He asked his bodyguard Channa what was wrong with him. 'He is ill', was the reply. 'Why is he ill?' asked the prince. 'That, my prince, is the way of life. All people become ill'. The prince looked thoughtful but said nothing.

The next day he came across an old man with a back bent like a bow, his head nodding and his hands trembling. Even with two sticks he was finding it hard to walk. 'Is this man also ill?' the prince asked Channa. 'No', replied Channa, 'he is old. That is what happens in old age'. Siddhartha looked thoughtful but again he said nothing.

The third sight was a funeral procession. A dead man was being carried to the burning ground to be cremated, according to Hindu custom, and his widow and children followed him weeping. Siddhartha asked Channa what was happening. 'This is the way of all flesh', he explained, 'whether prince or pauper, death comes for us all'. Again Siddhartha said nothing.

Siddhartha had witnessed the pain of sickness, old age and death. 'What is the cause of all this suffering?' he wondered. He had studied the Vedas, but all they told him was that it was the law of life, it was karma. As he sat in his palace pondering these mysteries, the sound of singing drifted through his window. But it only made him sadder. Pleasure was fleeting, he realised. It offered relief but could do nothing to slow the approach of death.

On the fourth day he went into the market place, Channa with him as usual. Among the shoppers and the merchants who supplied their needs, Siddhartha saw a monk in coarse robes, begging for food. He was old and obviously poor, yet he looked happy and serene. 'What kind of man is this?' he asked Channa. Channa explained that he was one of those who had left home to live without possessions and the cares they provoked.

Siddhartha returned to the comforts of his palace in deep thought. During that night, sleepless and troubled, he was hit by the realisation that *desire* was the cause of human suffering. Men and women were never content with their lot, never at peace. They craved what they did not possess. But no sooner was the desired object achieved than another craving took its place. The more he thought about it, the more desire revolted Siddhartha. It was a disease that afflicted everyone born into this world and there was no escape from its compulsions. But revolted though he was by desire, Siddhartha was also filled with compassion for those it tormented. It was then he decided to help them. He would find a way to release them from the clutches of desire so they would never again be born into this world of pain. He would search for the enlightenment that would deliver him from the turnings of the wheel of rebirth. Then he would guide others along the path he had found.

Having made his decision, Siddhartha rose from his bed. After whispering a silent farewell to his wife and son, he summoned Channa and out they rode into the night on his chariot pulled by the stallion Kanthaka. When they reached the edge of the forest Siddhartha stepped from the chariot and with his sword cut off his long black hair. He gave the hair to Channa and sent him back to the palace to show it as proof of the new life he had embarked upon. Then he swapped his costly robes for those of a tramp and set forth as a homeless pilgrim. Prince Siddhartha Gautama was twenty-nine years old when he became a beggar. This moment in his story is known as the Great Renunciation.

For six years he wandered, seeking the best way to purge the ache of desire and achieve enlightenment. Two approaches were offered by the sages he met. One was an intense form of mental exercise designed to discipline the mind and still its cravings. Siddhartha mastered the techniques and found them helpful. But they did not bring him the final release or enlightenment he was seeking. So he left the meditators and travelled on until he met a band of monks who practised ferocious austerity. The more intensely you deny your body, they told him, the clearer your mind will become. If you want to free your soul you must starve your body. Siddhartha then embarked on a programme of self-denial that brought him close to death. He said of himself at this time:

When I was living on a single fruit a day my body became emaciated ... my limbs became like the knotted joints of withered creepers ... like the rafters of a tumble-down roof were my gaunt ribs ... if I sought to feel my belly, it was my backbone which I found in my grasp.

He wondered to himself: surely if this theory of bodily renunciation were true I would have reached enlightenment by now because I have come to the very edge of death. Now so weak he was unable to drag his body any further, Siddhartha fainted. His friends thought he was about to die, but he recovered. And when he was back to himself he told the monks he had made a decision. Six years of intense meditation and renunciation had brought him no closer to the enlightenment he sought. So he was going to stop starving and torturing himself. Saddened by his announcement, the monks left him, and Siddhartha continued on his way alone.

He came to a wild fig tree and while he was resting beneath it he made a decision. Though my skin, nerves and bones may waste away and my life blood be dried up, he said to himself, I'll sit here until I attain enlightenment. After seven days it hit him that his desire to rid himself of desire was itself desire! He realised that his desire to be rid of desire had been the obstacle to his own enlightenment. As the meaning of this insight grew upon him, he became aware that he was now empty of desire. He passed into a state of ecstasy in which 'ignorance was destroyed, knowledge had arisen; darkness was destroyed, lightness had arisen'. Immediately he realised that 'Rebirth is no more; I have lived the highest life; my task is done; and now for me there is no more of what I have been'. The turning of the wheel of samsāra and rebirth ceased for him. It was then he became the Buddha, the Enlightened One. It is known as the Sacred Night.

Next he went looking for the monks he had disappointed by forsaking their path to enlightenment. He found them in the Deer Park at Benares, a city on the banks of the Ganges in northern India. In spite of his desertion, they received him courteously. His reply to their gentle accusation that by abandoning the life of mortification he had forfeited the possibility of enlightenment is known as the Sermon of the Turning of the Wheel. In this talk he again asked the question that had haunted him since he left home to search for enlightenment. What will bring an end to the turning of the wheel of samsāra onto which our cravings have chained us? The answer he gave was that the way out was by the path of moderation between extremes. He called it the Middle Path. 'There are two extremes, O monks, to avoid. One is a life of pleasure and its lusts; this is degrading . . . and without profit. The other is a life of self-torture; this is painful . . . and without profit. By avoiding these two extremes we gain the Middle Path which leads to Enlightenment'. And the signposts to the Middle Path were the Four Noble Truths. All life is permeated with suffering. The cause of suffering is desire. Desire can be eliminated. And the way to eliminate it is to follow the Eightfold Path.

The Buddha was a practical man, a man of action. A strong characteristic of practical people is their love of lists, things to do, things to remember, things to pick up at the market. Here's the Buddha's eightfold list of what's needed to eliminate the craving that causes suffering: right belief, right resolve, right speech, right behaviour, right occupation, right effort, right contemplation, right concentration. Right belief and right resolve are finding the Middle Path and following it. Next is the decision never to slander others or use coarse language. Even more important is the refusal to steal, kill or do anything shameful, and to avoid occupations that cause harm to others.

Buddhism is a practice, not a creed. It is something to do rather than something to believe. The key to its effectiveness is controlling the restless craving mind through meditation. By sitting still and watching how they breathe, by meditating on a word or a flower, practitioners move through different levels of consciousness to the calm that diminishes desire. Buddha would have agreed with an insight of the seventeenth-century French contemplative Blaise Pascal: 'all human evil comes from a single cause, man's inability to sit still in a room'. *A tendency that has probably gained us everything we have.*

After being convinced by the Buddha's exposition of the Middle Way, the monks became his followers and the Sangha, or order of

Buddhist monks and nuns, was born. Though the Buddha's teaching imposed no creed it was underpinned by the two assumptions of Indian religion, karma and samsāra: the Law of the Deed that leads to millions of rebirths. He taught that the quickest way to stop the wheel of rebirth turning was to become a monk and practise the disciplines that led to Enlightenment. But if your situation made that impossible, the next best thing was to live an ethical life in the hope that next time round you might attain a state in which assuming the ochre robe of the monk or nun might be possible.

For forty-five years after the Sermon at Benares the Buddha travelled and worked to strengthen his order of monks and nuns, the Sangha. As he neared death he told his followers that his leaving them did not matter because his teaching would remain, and it was the teaching that mattered. The prince who became the Buddha made his last journey to a town north-east of Benares. Feeling ill, he lay down between two trees and died. He was eighty years old. The religion Siddhartha Gautama founded spread throughout Asia and in time became a world religion, but it is hardly found today in the land of its birth. Unlike Jainism, which is found hardly anywhere else, and to which we next turn.

CHAPTER 6

Do No Harm

Like Buddhism, Jainism is an answer to the question Hinduism posed for humanity. If our present existence is only the latest of the many lives we shall lead because our karma has locked us onto the wheel of rebirth, how can we liberate ourselves and escape to a state called *nirvāṇa*? Nirvāna is a Sanskrit word meaning to be blown out like a candle. It is achieved when the soul finally escapes from samsāra. The Buddha's answer was to find the Middle Way between extremes. Jainism went in the opposite direction. It chose the most extreme way imaginable, the path of severe self-denial. And its highest ideal was for its followers to commit the act of *sallekhana* and starve themselves to death.

The word *Jainism* comes from a Sanskrit verb meaning to conquer. It refers to the battle Jains wage against their own nature to reach the enlightenment that brings salvation. In Jain tradition there have been twenty-four *jinas* or conquerors who achieved such mastery over their desires that they gained enlightenment. They became known as *tirthankaras*, meaning ford makers, because of their ability to lead souls across the river of rebirth to salvation on the other side. It is the last of these tirthankaras who is usually described as the 'founder' of Jainism. His name was Vardamana, though he was known as Mahavira, or great hero. Tradition tells us that he was born around 599 BCE in the Ganges basin of eastern India, the region that also saw the birth of Siddhartha Gautama who became the Buddha.

The Mahavira had more in common with the Buddha than just geography and chronology. He too was a prince. He too was obsessed with the problem of suffering and its causes. He too abandoned a privileged life to seek enlightenment. And he agreed with the Buddha that desire was the cause of suffering. People are unhappy because they crave what they do not possess; but no sooner do they get what they lusted after than they crave something else. It follows that since desire is the cause of suffering, only the extinction of desire can save us. And it was how he went about extinguishing desire that showed what a radical character Mahavira was. He said that release from the wheel of rebirth could only be achieved by avoiding evil and doing good. Like the Buddha, he too was a lover of lists. He distilled his method into Five Commandments. Do not kill or harm any living thing. Do not steal. Do not lie. Do not live an unchaste or undisciplined life. Do not covet or crave anything.

At first glance there is nothing new in these rules. Many other systems offer the same list. What is distinctive about Jainism is the depth it gives to Mahavira's first commandment not to kill or harm other creatures. *Ahimsa*, or non-violence, is the main feature of his teaching. And he makes it absolute and universal. Only by absolute non-violence can those seeking salvation change the karma that clamps them to the wheel of rebirth.

Jain monks and nuns are not to hurt or kill *anything*! They are not to kill animals for food. They are not to hunt or fish. Nor are they to swat the mosquito that bites them on the cheek or the bee that stings them on the neck. If they find a spider or any other unwanted insect in the house they are not to squash it. If they don't want it around they are to capture it carefully, making sure they do not injure it, and release it reverently outdoors. And because the

very ground on which they walk is teeming with tiny living creatures, they must walk carefully to avoid harming them. To be sure
their heavy tread will not crush the life beneath their feet, Jains
fashion a broom of soft feathers and gently sweep the path in front
of them as they make their way over it. Some even wear masks over
their mouths to avoid harming insects by inhaling them. Their
reverence and respect for all forms of life even applies to root
vegetables. They are not to be pulled from the earth and eaten.
They too are creatures whose lives are as valuable as humans.

So if they wouldn't eat meat, fish or vegetables, how did Jains
survive? Some of them actually chose not to. Sallekhana, or suicide
by starvation, was the highest Jain ideal. It marked the extinction
of desire in the soul and its final liberation from karma. But you
only have to think about it for a moment to realise that suicide was
unlikely to become a universal practice, even among Jains. Religions
all have their different levels of intensity, from the red heat of the
zealot to the occasional observance of the lukewarm. Jainism,
though one of the hottest religions in history, also had different
temperature levels among its practitioners. Most of them didn't
starve themselves to death. But what they did was extreme enough.
They survived on fruit, but only fruit that had fallen to the ground.
Jains were radical fruitarians. By confining themselves to windfalls
they sustained themselves without harming any other forms of life.

Apart from its belief in the sacredness of all forms of life, Jainism
burdened itself with very little religious theory. It had no place for
a supreme god or creator in its system. And it rejected the cruelties
of the caste system. But its route to salvation did depend on a
precise map of the universe. Jains believed the universe consisted
of two gigantic spheres joined by a tiny waist. To picture it, imagine
twisting a knot in the middle of an inflated balloon, turning it into
two parts connected by your knot. In Jainism the knot in the
middle was our world, where souls did their time on the wheel of
rebirth. And just as too much food made their bodies heavy and
difficult to drag around, so Jains believed bad behaviour added
weight to the soul and made it harder to get off the wheel of
rebirth. Souls who lived bad lives came back for the next round in

a lower form. Maybe as a snake or a frog. Maybe even as a carrot or an onion. The souls who lived truly evil lives became so heavy their weight pulled them down into the seven hells in the bottom sphere of the universe, where each hell was more terrible in its torments than the one above it.

By the same law, souls who purged themselves of sin got lighter the harder they struggled. Really dedicated Jains practised what is called extreme *asceticism*, a word from Greek athletics that means to train so rigorously that one outclasses all others in the field. The jinas, the top athletes of Jainism, worked so hard that their souls became light enough to float higher and higher through the heavens of the top sphere. When they made it to the twenty-sixth heaven they had reached nirvāna and the end of all their struggles. They were now forever in a state of motionless bliss. Salvation at last!

Another interesting aspect of Jainism was the way it extended its struggle for weightlessness into the realm of ideas. As well as wrong acts, wrong ideas could weigh down the soul. History certainly shows that disagreement over ideas, including religious ideas, is one of the main causes of violence between humans. For Jains, the doctrine of ahimsa or non-violence applied to the approach they took to people's ideas as well as to their bodies. Even in the life of the mind Jains were to do no harm and act non-violently. They respected the different ways humans saw and experienced reality, while recognising that no one ever saw the whole of it.

They called this doctrine of respect *anekantavada.* And to illustrate it they told a story about six blind men who were invited to describe an elephant by feeling different parts of its body. The man who felt a leg said the elephant was like a pillar. The one who felt the tail said it was like a rope. The one who felt the trunk said the elephant was like the branch of a tree. The man who explored the ear said the elephant was like a hand fan. The one who moved his hands over the belly said it was like a wall. And the one who felt the tusk said the elephant was like a solid pipe. Their teacher told them they were all correct in their descriptions of the elephant, yet each had grasped only a part and not the whole. The moral of the story was that humans were all limited in their grasp of reality. They may not be entirely blind to it, but they can only see it from a single angle. That was OK as long as they didn't claim their view was the whole picture and force others to see things the same way.

For Jains, the limitation of our knowledge was a consequence of the unreality in which we were trapped in our fallen existence. Only the enlightened achieved perfect knowledge. Whatever we make of other aspects of Jainism, its encouragement of spiritual modesty is rare in religion. Religions like to think they've got the last word on things. They reject the thought that they are all blind beggars squabbling over the shape of an elephant.

Mahavira travelled through India preaching his message and attracting disciples. By the time of his death by self-starvation in 527 BCE, when he was seventy years old, he had a following of fourteen thousand monks and thirty-six thousand nuns. Monks and nuns were the real athletes of Jainism. They trained hard to make themselves light enough to achieve nirvāna in their present lifetime. And they gathered Mahavira's sermons on non-violence and reverence for all life in their sacred book the *Agamas.*

Most religions fracture into different sects once they are well established, with each sect claiming to be the true version of the original prophet or teacher. Jainism was no exception. It split into two groups, but their differences were mild and actually quite endearing. One group, who called themselves the *Digambaras* (meaning sky-clad), insisted that monks and nuns shouldn't wear any clothes. While the other group, the *Svetambaras* (white-clad), allowed them to wear white robes.

In addition to its monks and nuns, Jainism still has millions of lay followers in India. Though its monks and nuns are its real athletes, its lay members live as simple a life as their place in society makes possible. They don't expect to reach the twenty-sixth heaven in a single lifetime of struggle. But they hope their current life of non-violent gentleness will guarantee them a place as a monk or nun next time round. And it will be after that life that they will finally reach nirvāna.

Given the nature of Jainism, it was never going to become a mass religion, but it has been an influential one. And it introduces us to an interesting distinction. While extreme practices may only ever have a minority appeal, they can have an effect on majority opinion and soften its attitudes. Jain thinking on the sacredness of all life has contributed to the vegetarian movement in its various forms. And its doctrine of ahimsa or non-violence has had a significant impact on politics. It influenced Mahatma Gandhi, the lawyer who led the campaign for independence from British rule in India in the first half of the twentieth century. It influenced Martin Luther King, the Christian preacher who led the campaign for civil rights for African Americans in the USA in the second half of the century.

And Jainism continues to lay before us the truth that desire is the cause of much human suffering and only in learning to control it does our happiness and contentment lie. Few of us will want to go sky-clad or starve ourselves to death, but the thought of those who do may just prompt us all to live a bit more simply.

I pointed out at the beginning of this book that it would be impossible to follow a strictly chronological route in tracing the emergence of the different religions. That was because place is as important as time in this story. Different things happened at the same time in different places. So we'd have to zigzag our way through history. That's why in the next chapter we'll zig back in time to a few hundred years after the Aryans invaded India and zag West in place to look at one of the most important figures in the history of religion, a mysterious character called Abraham.

CHAPTER 7

The Wanderer

Ur. It's a short two-letter word. The 'u' is pronounced as in 'up'. The 'r' is rolled the way a Scot would pronounce it. So it is Ur – or Urrrr. And it is where one of the most important figures in the history of religion was born some time around 1800 BCE – the patriarch Abraham. Abraham is claimed by Jews, Christians and Muslims as their founding father. Think of a tiny stream trickling out of a distant mountain that becomes three mighty rivers thousands of miles away on a vast plain, and you'll get the idea. Ur was in the south-east of Mesopotamia, a Greek name that means 'between two rivers', the rivers being the Tigris and the Euphrates. Ur was in the country we now call Iraq.

According to the story that has come down to us, Abraham was the son of Terah. He had two brothers, Nahor and Haran. In the Bible we find their story in the book of Genesis. But an old teaching guide to the Hebrew Bible has more stories about them. It tells us they were shepherds, pasturing sheep in the lush meadows of the Euphrates valley. And Terah had a profitable sideline making statues or idols of the gods worshipped by the people of the region.

The Mesopotamians had four top gods. Anu was the god of heaven, Ki the goddess of the earth, Enlil god of the air and Eki god of water. The sun and the moon were also worshipped as gods. It's worth noting how in ancient religion the forces of nature were almost automatically thought of as divine.

Like the people of India, the inhabitants of Mesopotamia wanted something to look at when they made their devotions to the gods, and Terah was happy to oblige them from his idol workshop. One day when he was absent and Abraham was in charge of the business an old man came in to buy an idol. 'How old are you?' asked Abraham. 'Seventy', said the old man. 'Then you're an idiot', Abraham replied. 'You were born seven decades ago, yet you're going to worship an idol that was made in the workshop at the back of this shop only yesterday!' The old man pondered a moment, declined the purchase, took back his money and left the shop.

His brothers were furious when they heard what had happened. They warned their father that Abraham was endangering the family business with his strong opinions. So Terah banned Abraham from the front of the shop and ordered him instead to perform the role of receiving the offerings brought by customers to their favourite gods in the room where they were on display. One day a woman arrived with a gift of food for one of the gods. Instead of proffering it to the idol in the customary way, Abraham mocked her. 'It has a mouth all right', he said, 'but it can neither eat the meal you prepared for it nor say thank you afterwards. It has hands, but they can't pick up a single morsel of the food you've laid before it. And though it has beautifully carved feet, it couldn't take a single step towards you. As far as I am concerned, those who made it and those who worship it are as stupid and useless as the thing itself.'

This was dangerous talk for two reasons. Challenging the settled religion of a community is never a popular thing to do. But it's made worse if the criticism also threatens the local economy. This was a society that worshipped many gods, and the manufacture of images of those same gods was a profitable industry. Abraham had landed himself in trouble. The safest thing to do was to leave. From this moment he became a wanderer who trekked great distances with his family and herds. But it was his spiritual journey that made religious history.

Abraham's story marks the beginning of the shift from polytheism to monotheism, from the relaxed worship of many gods to strict adherence to one. What prompted it? Why was Abraham so angry at those harmless little statues in his father's shop? We have to use our imagination to get into Abraham's mind, but it's easy to figure out part of what was going on there. He'd watched his father carve these little images. He knew what went into their making. So how could he possibly rate them as anything other than human toys? But why didn't he just shrug his shoulders at how gullible people were and move on? Why did he get so angry?

It was because he was a prophet who heard the voice of God speaking to him in his head. And the voice warned him that worshipping these gods was not just a game that kept people entertained and idol makers in business. It was based on a terrible and dangerous lie. There was only one God! And he did not just disdain the idols and images of the gods; he hated them, because they prevented his children from coming to know their own father. Like a parent whose children had been stolen by strangers, he wanted them back and those who had kidnapped them punished.

This is an important turning point in the human story and it's worth another moment's thought. It is obvious from our history that humans are good at hating each other. And it is usually those who differ from us in some way who become the objects of our hatred. Race, class, colour, sex, politics, even hair colour can prompt ugly behaviour in us. So can religion. In fact, religious hatred is probably the deadliest form of this human disease, because it gives human dislike divine justification. It is one thing to hate people because you don't like their opinions. It is another thing to say God hates them too and wants them exterminated. So it is worth noticing how intense religious conviction can add a dangerous element to human relationships – as another incident from Abraham's story will remind us.

As well as telling him to hate idols, the voice in Abraham's head ordered him to leave his father's country and migrate to another

land where in time he was to become a great nation. So Genesis
tells us that Abraham set out with his family, his flocks and herds,
and travelled west across the Euphrates till he came to the land of
Canaan. Canaan, known today as Israel or Palestine, lay on the
eastern edge of the Great Sea, which we now call the Mediterranean.
Abraham settled not on the coast but inland along the limestone
ridge that forms the spine of the country. And there his family with
their flocks and herds prospered.

Then one day the voice in Abraham's head spoke to him again.
It told him to take his son Isaac to a local mountain where he was
to offer him as a sacrifice to God. Abraham was used to killing
animals and burning them as gifts for God, but he had never before
been commanded to kill one of his own children. But he dared not
question the order. He rose early the next morning, roped a pile of
firewood onto his ass, and set out with his son and two young men.
When he reached the foot of the mountain he told the young men
to stay behind and guard the ass. He tied the pile of firewood onto
Isaac's back, lit a flaming torch, shoved a sharp knife in his belt, and
the two of them set off up the mountain. As they trudged up the
trail Isaac spoke to his father: 'You have fire and knife ready for the
sacrifice, father, but where's the animal you're going to slaughter?'
'Don't worry, my son', replied Abraham, 'God will provide what we
need.'

When they reached the place on the mountain where the sacrifice was to be offered, Abraham arranged some stones into a make-
shift altar and spread the firewood on top of it. Then he took hold
of his trembling son and bound him to the firewood face down. He
grabbed Isaac's long hair and yanked his head back to expose his
throat. Then he pulled the knife from his belt and was about to slit
his son's throat when the voice in his head called to him again.

'Abraham, do not slay your son', it said. 'Your willingness to kill
him at my command proves that your loyalty to me is stronger
than your human affections. So I'll spare your son.' Shaking
convulsively, Abraham lowered the knife. Then he caught sight of
a ram whose horns were tangled in a bush. In a frenzy of relief he
tore open its throat and offered it to God on the altar instead of his

Psycho

son. We are never told what Isaac made of this terrifying scene on Mount Moriah, but it's not hard to imagine.

We know that human sacrifice was practised in some early religions. And it's not hard to understand how it started. If gods are thought of as unpredictable rulers who have to be kept onside, you can see how the primitive mind might conclude that as well as giving them the best animals an occasional human sacrifice might really win some favour. There may be a distant echo of that grim history in the Abraham and Isaac story. But that is not how it has been interpreted in traditional Judaism, Christianity and Islam, for all of which it is a key text. What it exemplifies for them is absolute subjection to the will of God above all earthly ties. While we would now judge as insane a man who claimed God told him to kill his son – even if he relented at the last minute – this does not mean we have to decide that all religion is madness. But it will be wise to place a question mark against some of its claims as we follow its stories through time. The danger we have noticed here is the tendency to give too much authority to the voice of God speaking in the human mind. Abraham's hatred of idols is a good guide here.

We followed his thinking in his dismissal of idols as human creations that it was absurd to treat as divine. But aren't our *ideas* about God also human inventions? We might not have crafted them with our hands out of bits of wood and stone, but we did form them in our minds out of words and ideas. That should make us cautious about the claims that are made for them. We have already seen how dangerous some of them can be. The idea that the gods may want us to sacrifice our children to them shows that religion can be an enemy of the human community. God's test of Abraham proves, if nothing else, that humans can persuade themselves to do almost anything if they think the order has come from 'on high'. And almost everything has been done in the name of religion at one time or another.

I said that the story of Abraham was a turning-point in the history of religion. It moved men and women away from polytheism to monotheism and to the idea of a single god. And it showed that religions were never static. They constantly evolved and changed. Religion was a moving picture. That is why Abraham is such a compelling figure. He wandered and changed direction not only on the face of the earth but in his own mind. That ability to turn around and change direction is one of the marks of all interesting human beings. And it is one of the keys to the understanding of religion.

Abraham was a wanderer, and after his death, the people he founded continued to migrate as people have always done in their search for a better life. The story says that some generations after the death of Abraham a great famine hit the land of Canaan and it prompted his descendants to take to the road again. This time they went south across another great river into Egypt, where the next chapter in their history opened. And we'll reacquaint ourselves with Moses.

CHAPTER 8

In the Bulrushes

Isaac, the son Abraham came close to killing at the command of the voice in his head, survived to become a father himself. And Isaac's son Jacob, like his grandfather before him, heard the voice of God addressing him. It told him that he was no longer to be called Jacob. His new name was to be Israel, meaning 'God rules'. So his twelve sons were called the children of Israel or Israelites. Like his grandfather Abraham, Jacob, now called Israel, was a wandering herdsman. He led his flocks from place to place in search of water and good grazing. Over the years the Israelites grew as a tribe who were able to hold their own against other tribes, competing with them for the best pastures and the most abundant wells.

But in time a great famine hit the land of Canaan. The grass withered and the wells dried, so the Israelites decided, as people have done since time began, that they'd better try their luck somewhere else. They migrated south to Egypt where the river Nile fed lush pasturelands for their herds to graze in. At first the Egyptians were welcoming and allowed them to settle in the Province of Goshen in the north-east of the country, close to the Nile and not far from the sea. Here the Israelites prospered and their numbers grew. But they kept to themselves. Remembering Abraham's contempt for idols, they held themselves aloof from the local religion, a lively form of polytheism in which gods were worshipped in the shapes of dogs, cats, crocodiles and other animals.

As often happens to people who refuse to blend in with the majority, the Israelites became increasingly unpopular among the Egyptians. And as they grew in numbers and became more successful the dislike they provoked turned into hatred. Then the hatred turned to persecution and forced labour. And when even this organised harshness failed to suppress them, the Egyptian authorities decided on a policy of planned destruction. To force the daughters of Israel to take Egyptian partners and be merged into the general population, the king decreed that all newborn male Israelites were to be killed at birth. One mother decided that she would rather give her newborn son away than see him slaughtered. So she placed him in a carefully waterproofed basket and left him in the reeds on the banks of the Nile at a spot where she knew the daughter of the Pharaoh, the Egyptian king, came to bathe. The ruse worked. When the king's daughter came upon the baby floating in the bulrushes she adopted him as her own and gave him the Egyptian name Moses.

Though he led a life of privilege in the royal palace of the Pharaohs, Moses was aware that he was an Israelite and not an Egyptian. He had a growing sense that his destiny lay with the slaves and not with their oppressors who had adopted him. So he was curious to see what was happening to them. One day his curiosity drew him to watch a band of them at work. When he saw one of the Egyptian gang bosses beating up one of the Israelites, he was so enraged that he killed him and buried him in the sand. Interest drew him out again the next day. But this time his anger was provoked by the sight of two Israelites fighting. The one who had started the fight jeered at him when he tried to interfere. 'I suppose you'll now kill me the way you got rid of the Egyptian yesterday and hide me in the sand as well!' Realising he was discovered and that word would soon reach the palace and put him in danger,

Moses fled into the desert where he was given shelter by a family of shepherds.

This is where we first encountered him, kneeling before a thorn-bush, listening to a voice that spoke words to him he didn't want to hear and calling him to a dangerous duty he did not want to under-take. It was the same voice that had commanded Abraham to risk his life by denouncing the gods worshipped by the Mesopotamians. It was the same voice that had ordered Abraham to offer his son Isaac as a sacrifice. And it was the same voice that had commanded Jacob to change his name to Israel or 'God rules'.

This was a new way of thinking about the gods. It was accepted that every tribe and people had their own gods. The idea that a single god controlled human destiny, and maybe even history itself, was new and frightening. When Moses had asked the name of the one who had spoken to him the answer had been even more disconcerting. 'I AM' was the reply. It was hard to figure out exactly what that meant, but it suggested the voice was the source of all life, the energy and meaning behind everything that existed. And those to whom it spoke sensed that getting involved with it would place them in danger.

Not that it had given them any say in the matter. It had turned up out of nowhere and thundered into their minds like an inescap-able idea. It told them there was only *one* god, could only *be* one god. All other gods were human creations, formed either by human imaginations or fashioned literally by human hands. These so-called gods were lies. And lies damaged the human spirit and had to be cast aside. It was the one and only true god who had chosen the children of Israel to proclaim that truth to the world. No wonder those to whom this message came were afraid. The world was full of gods with hordes of enthusiastic worshippers and the businesses they had established to serve them. Insulting people's beliefs was bad enough; threatening the way they earned their living was even worse.

That's why Moses tried to resist the voice's demands. He had just made his escape from Egypt and its rulers. And now the voice in his head was telling him to go back and organise a rebellion! He was to lead the Israelites, whom he already knew to be an ungrateful and unruly mob, out of Egypt to another country. Who knew what kind of welcome they would find in the land promised to them, supposing they ever got there? But the voice was insistent and Moses reluctantly obeyed. Back he went to Egypt to face two trials. The greater challenge was to persuade the Israelites that the God of Abraham, Isaac and Jacob had commanded him to lead them out of Egypt to a new land, back where they'd come from generations ago. Grumbling, they agreed to follow him if he could persuade Pharaoh to release them. And how did he intend to do that?

Moses' first approach was to ask the Egyptians to give the Israelites a few days off to worship their god in the desert north of Goshen. Already contemptuous of the proud and exclusive religion of the Israelites, the Egyptians refused to let them have a holiday to serve their jealous god. The story then tells us that there followed a prolonged campaign orchestrated by Moses in which the god of the Israelites struck the Egyptians with one disaster after another. It culminated in a horrifying echo of the slaughter of the sons of Israel that had catapulted Moses into the household of Pharaoh.

The voice told Moses to command the Israelites to stay at home behind locked doors on a night it had set. Each family was to sacrifice a lamb and dab its blood on their doorposts as a sign that it was an Israelite and not an Egyptian household. And that midnight God went through the land killing the first-born child of every family as well as the first-born of their cattle, but passing over the houses marked with blood and leaving them unscathed. When morning came terrible cries pierced the day. There was not an Egyptian house in which someone had not died during the night. So Pharaoh summoned Moses and said 'You win, take your people into the desert for a few days to serve your god. And leave us to mourn our dead.' The great escape was on.

Moses led the Israelites in a long straggle of humans and animals over a dangerous estuary known as the Sea of Reeds close to the shore of the Mediterranean. The tide was out and they made it safely to the other side. But by that time it had dawned on the Egyptians that they had been duped. The Israelites were not away for a few days on a brief religious pilgrimage. If that's all they were up to they wouldn't have taken all their flocks and herds with them. No, they were escaping for ever and they had already stolen a day's march on them. So the Egyptians mounted their chariots and pursued them. They reached the estuary of the Sea of Reeds just as the tide was flooding back in. They were caught in the rush of water and all of them were drowned. The Israelites celebrated this as an act of God. At last they were away free and clear.

This was the defining event in the history of the Jews and it has been observed by them with due solemnity ever since. Called the Feast of the Passover, the annual festival looks back to the night the Divine Destroyer passed over the children of Israel and spared them for their escape from bondage in Egypt into their own promised land. On the eve of the feast Jewish children ask their parents why the Passover differs from all the other meals they enjoy.

Why do they eat matzos – flat unleavened bread – instead of normal bread on this night? They are told it is to remind them that on the eve of their escape from Egypt there was no time to wait for the leavened bread to rise into fully baked loaves. They had to take it out of the oven just as it came. When they ask why instead of a variety of vegetables on this night they must eat bitter herbs to go with the meal, they are told it is to remind them of the bitterness of their years of slavery in Egypt. Dipping the herbs once in salt water and once in a sweet paste they are reminded that their tears were turned into joy and their pains to pleasure. And when they ask why on this night they recline at table, they are told that in Egypt it was only the free that reclined, while slaves had to stand. Now they are free so they too can now recline!

These questions have been asked by Jewish children on Passover Eve for more than 3,300 years. The same questions asked and the same answers given. They are free so now they can recline when they eat! The poignancy in this story is that, countless times in their history, when Jewish children asked these questions and heard the answers that announced their freedom, they were again in captivity. That is the cloud that has shadowed this story as it has moved through time. It celebrated a great act of liberation as the defining moment of a people whose history has been one of confinement and persecution.

But it teaches an important lesson about how religion works. Religious stories may look back to the past but they are actually meant to give hope for the future. That was how the Jewish people used this story. They looked back on the Exodus as their date of birth as a people. But what came next was not an Independence Day celebration with fireworks and lots of feasting. It was a long and miserable trek through the desert in search of a better future.

CHAPTER 9

The Ten Commandments

The children of Israel had escaped from bondage in Egypt, but their troubles were just beginning. The drowning of the Egyptian army in the Sea of Reeds had given them courage and Moses had persuaded them to follow him out into the desert. But they never really understood what he was talking about when it came to God. The general view at the time was that gods, like football teams today, were ten a penny. You obviously supported the home god, but that didn't mean you despised all the others. You knew that in the god league there were many players. The Israelites knew there was something special about the god who had spoken to Moses, but to them that didn't mean there were no other gods in the league. It meant theirs was the best because it was *theirs*!

It didn't take them long to find out that Moses didn't see things that way. He had told them he was leading them to a land flowing with milk and honey, but he seemed in no hurry to get them there. Ages after they left Egypt, they came to the foot of a mountain. Wait here, he said, while I go to the top to get the next set of directions from the voice of God. He was away so long the Israelites got bored and restless, so the men in charge decided to divert them with a religious festival. They got the craftsmen among them to make an enormous golden bull calf, one of the symbols for God in the religion of Egypt. They raised it up on a platform and called the Israelites to worship it. Maybe they were already feeling homesick for Egypt. Or maybe they just needed a break after their long trudge through the desert. The worship of the golden calf became a rave. The drums beat and the Israelites danced excitedly round the image yelling their heads off, as ecstatic as fans at a rock concert.

Suddenly Moses was back in their midst and he was furious. He stopped the revelry and called for silence. The voice that had spoken to him on the mountain had sent him back with a list of Ten Commandments the Israelites were to follow *starting now*!

Most of the commandments made sense for any community that wanted to hold itself together. No killing. No stealing. No cheating on your spouse. No lying. A day off for workers. Sensible stuff like that. The First Commandment also made sense. The god who had led them out of Egypt was to be their only god and they were to have no other. They were OK with that. You had to support the home side.

What surprised the Israelites was the Second Commandment. It forbade them making pictures, not just of God but of anything. No images! No art! That baffled them. It was as natural as breathing for humans to paint the animals they hunted or the gods they worshipped, as any child with a piece of chalk could prove. The voice that spoke to Moses was deeply suspicious of any kind of art, but it became absolutely furious when humans tried to use it to capture the mystery of its own being. So what lay behind God's fury?

To get hold of the issue it will help if we go back to our discussion of symbols. We noticed how they connected people to bigger realities: the way a piece of coloured cloth could stand for a whole country. Symbols are among humanity's most useful inventions, a short-hand way of capturing big abstract subjects such as the idea of a nation. And when writing was invented they became even more useful. You could now translate anything into words in a book you could hold in your hands. The mistake was to confuse the words with what they stood for and treat them as if they were the same. Things are never what we *say* they are. You can't drink the word water. It's the sign *for* water, not *water itself.*

The trouble is that believers often treat religious words as if that rule didn't apply to them. It was as if their words for God *were* God. Their books weren't ink marks on paper but God himself compressed between covers. No wonder they often ended up fighting with each other over who had the best words and the best symbols for God. None of them comes close, thundered the God of the Second Commandment. No human art of any sort, whether in the form of pictures on a wall or words in a book gets anywhere near conveying the mystery of God.

The Second Commandment was the most important insight into God ever discovered by humans. Its real target was religion. And not just the kind that got people dancing round a golden calf. It was warning us that no religious system could capture or contain the mystery of God. Yet in history, as we'll see, that's exactly what many of them would go on to claim. The Second Commandment was an early warning that the organisations that claimed to speak for God would become God's greatest rivals, the most dangerous idols of all. But it would take the Israelites a long time to get the message.

After that rave in the desert round the golden calf it was time to move on. There was a Promised Land to win. Moses got them within sight of it. The voice of God told him to climb a mountain to see it from afar. And it was there that Moses died. So it was his general Joshua who led the invasion. But it was no walkover. Even after they had planted themselves in the land they had to wage continuous warfare against all the local tribes to keep their hold. So the Israelites decided they needed a king to lead them in this incessant warfare. The other tribes had kings so why couldn't they? Their first king was Saul and he spent most of his reign fighting to secure Israel's place in Canaan.

One of the tribes they came up against was the Philistines. And among their fierce soldiers was a giant called Goliath. One day when the two armies were lined up against each other, Goliath stepped forward to challenge anyone from Saul's army to single combat. No one volunteered from Israel's side till a young shepherd boy stepped forward to accept the challenge. But they scoffed at him. How could a lad like him take on a trained killer like Goliath? 'The same way I have protected my father's sheep from wolves', replied the boy, 'with my sling'. He stepped out to face the giant, who advanced on him with a roar. As Goliath drew his arm back to throw his spear, the shepherd boy calmly put a stone in his sling, swung it round once and let it fly. It struck Goliath on the temple and knocked him out. The boy then used the giant's own sword to behead him. Saul's army had won the day and the Israelites had a new hero. His name was David.

When Saul died in battle David succeeded him and became the king Israel would look back on as their ideal. He reigned for thirty years, much of it spent in battle. It was his son Solomon who built Israel's first temple, where the people offered God their finest beasts in sacrifice and the best crops of their fields. And they smothered him behind flattering clouds of incense. They had come a long way from their days of bondage in Egypt. They were no longer a loose alliance of wandering tribes. Now they were a proper nation. They had their own king. They had a fine temple. They'd finally made it. Except their God didn't think so!

So the voice that had spoken to Moses began to speak again. It had been silent for generations but it thundered now into the minds of a new generation of prophets. The voice told them how much it hated what the Israelites had turned him into. Their liberator had become a greedy idol like one of the gods of the people they had displaced. That wasn't what he wanted. He wanted justice for the poor. He wanted widows and orphans cared for, not cheated out of their possessions. Above all he wanted the Israelites to recover the simplicity of life they had known in the desert when they had all looked after each other. But it would take another period of slavery in a foreign land for the Israelites finally to understand what God had been trying to tell them all along.

As an independent kingdom they had never been very secure anyway. Even after they'd won their battles against the local tribes and had made the land of Canaan their own, they had been in constant danger. Their Promised Land was a corridor between mighty powers to the north and to the south. Egypt in the south they knew about. They had history there. But it was the Assyrian Empire to the north in Mesopotamia that had the biggest impact on their freedom. And hundreds of years after the Exodus had liberated them from Egypt the Israelites were again in bondage. They were overrun by the Assyrians and suppressed as a kingdom. More than 10,000 of them were deported and sent into exile in Babylon. And just as their idea of God had been changed by their triumphs in Canaan, so was it changed again by their sufferings in Babylon.

At first they thought they had lost their God forever. He was in the temple Solomon had built for him back in Jerusalem. They wept by the waters of Babylon when they remembered it. How could they sing the Lord's song in a strange land? But their grief brought them a new understanding of God. God was not an idol stuck in a temple. He wasn't even stuck in Canaan. God was everywhere! God was with them in Babylon as he had been with them in Jerusalem. And in Egypt! In fact, God had been with them at all times and in all places, just as the prophets had said. They could see it all now. If only they had understood what the prophets had told them! But they would make up for it now.

They began to collect the stories that had come down to them about God's actions in their past: stories about the voice that had spoken to Abraham, Isaac, Jacob and Moses; stories about their escape from Egypt and settlement in the land of Canaan; stories about how they had been called into a covenant or marriage with the one true god who would be with them always, whether in bondage or in freedom, whether in their own land with its beloved rivers and hills, or in this land whose rivers and whose language were strange to them. These were the thoughts that came to them in their exile in Babylon as they wondered about the meaning of their own history. God began speaking to them again through the prophets he sent. And this time they listened.

CHAPTER 10

Prophets

Prophets are not *fore-tellers*. They are *forth-tellers*. They don't predict the future so much as set forth or announce what they hear from God. Abraham heard the voice of God mocking the idols of the Mesopotamians. Moses heard it summoning him to become the liberator of the Israelites from Egypt and lead them to the Promised Land. And when the children of Israel had settled in Canaan and kings ruled over them the voice of God did not fall silent. It was heard by simple men who stepped out of obscurity and challenged the powerful for not keeping the law God had given to Moses on the Holy Mountain. The prophets were compelling speakers who used stories to get their message across. And even kings were not spared their attention. Here's a story about how a prophet challenged Israel's greatest king, David, whom we last met killing the giant Goliath with a sling and a stone.

David came to the throne of Israel around 1000 BCE. He chose a fortified hill called Mount Zion on which to build his capital Jerusalem or City of Peace, a beautiful city that is still sacred to millions today. Though David was a great warrior and a charismatic leader, he was a far from perfect man. One day a prophet called Nathan came to tell him about a recent outrage. There was a rich man in the countryside who owned thousands of sheep and cattle and wanted for nothing. One of his tenants was a poor man whose only possession was a little ewe lamb that he loved like a daughter. When an unexpected guest arrived at the rich man's house, rather than slaughtering one of his own sheep he took the poor man's lamb and cooked it for his guest.

When King David heard the story he leapt to his feet and demanded: 'Who is this monster?' 'You are the man', replied Nathan. Nathan knew that David had slept with Bathsheba the wife of Uriah, a loyal soldier in his army, away on a campaign at the time. To keep his offence secret David arranged to have Uriah killed in battle. Then he had married Bathsheba quietly. Because of Nathan's challenge, David admitted his crime and tried to make amends. Prophets knew the power of stories to make people change the direction of their lives. But not all their stories were designed to confront them with God's displeasure. Sometimes, as well as a telling-off, they offered consolation and hope for the future. Here's one of them.

About four hundred years after David's death, when the Israelites were exiled in Babylon and sat in despair remembering their beloved Jerusalem, one of the exiles brought them a message he had received from God. His name was Ezekiel. At first he scolded them about their past. God had not called them out of captivity in Egypt so that they would end up like all the other nations. Other nations wanted to be rich and successful and swagger on the world's stage. And they used their gods to help get them there. Religion for them was just a branch of politics.

Well, Israel's God was not an idol to be exploited by politicians in their power games. Nor were they to be a nation like the other nations. They were to be a holy nation, whose sole purpose on earth was to serve their God. But they had let themselves be sucked into the power games of the region. So God had punished them by exiling them in Babylon.

Ezekiel's blaming of the exile on Israel's sins introduced another interesting idea into the history of religion. Every time the people of Israel suffered from the power struggles of the region in which they lived, the prophets blamed their pain not on the armies that trampled over them but on their unfaithfulness to God. The idea was born that if bad things happened to you it wasn't tough luck, it was punishment for your sins. And since bad things kept happening to Israel they were constantly being chided by the prophets for their sinfulness. But there were times when God stopped chiding and started comforting Israel. And one of the most moving messages of consolation came to them through Ezekiel.

Ezekiel not only heard voices, he saw visions. And one of his visions contained a message of hope for captive Israel. In his vision he stood on a hill looking into a wide valley filled with dry bones. The voice told him to prophesy to the bones and tell them that breath would enter them, flesh would clothe them and they would live again. So he did as he had been instructed. Immediately there was a sound of rattling as the bones all joined together and the valley was filled with human skeletons. Next, sinews, flesh and skin grew over the bare skeletons, and the valley was filled with dead bodies. At last, breath came into the bodies and they stood up. And it was as if a great army of vibrant warriors filled the valley. These bones, the voice told Ezekiel, were the Israelites who thought their lives were over and they were dead and buried in Babylon. But God would soon restore them to life and bring them back to their own land of Israel.

That's exactly what happened. In 539 BCE the Persians defeated the Assyrians and the Persian king Cyrus sent the exiles back to Israel and told them to rebuild the temple wrecked by the Assyrians and restore their religious traditions. And for the next two hundred years the Israelites were left to their own religious devices. Now, at last, they began to live up to the meaning of their name: God rules. They saw themselves not as just another nation led by human leaders, but as a religious community ruled by God, a *theocracy*. And they set about rebuilding the temple that was to be the symbol of God's presence among them, the very centre of their existence. The temple was finished and dedicated in 515 BCE.

There was no longer a king in Israel, so the high priest of the temple became the most important person in the land. He was seen as God's representative on earth. And it was during this long process of consolidation that something died that had been part of their history since Abraham. Prophecy ceased! Now, instead of living prophets who brought the constant surprise of a new word of God to the Israelites, books were compiled that gathered together the stories of their God-guided history and the laws that were to govern their lives from now on.

The most important of these were the first five books of the Bible, called the Pentateuch or Five Scrolls, a papyrus scroll being the substance on which the old scribes would have written. It was during this period of peace after their return from exile that the story of Israel's long relationship with God was finally committed to writing. And from being a people of the Voice they became the people of the Book.

In its early years there had been an experimental feel to the religion of the Israelites. We might even describe it as freelance religion. It was driven not by professional clerics but by gifted amateurs who heard God speaking to them directly. That's how all religions start. They begin when people with special gifts, the ones we call prophets or sages, start hearing voices and seeing visions. They tell others what they have seen and what they have heard. Those who have not seen the visions or heard the voices respond with belief to what they have been told. And religious structures begin to grow.

As these structures become more elaborate, a new type of leader is needed. And the move from the amateur to the professional begins. Teachers are needed to interpret the sacred stories that have been stitched together. Priests are needed to preside at the festivals that celebrate the events recorded in the book. Temples are needed where all of this activity can be concentrated. And when this long process is complete, the world has another fully fledged religion to add to its collection.

But a sense remains that something was lost along the way, which is why religions always look back to their early years with both longing and regret. Like couples who get bored living together once the passion of their early love has faded, they look back with longing to the days when it flowed effortlessly. This is why all religions spend a lot of time looking back to their early years in an attempt to rekindle that original burning love. But it's hard going, because the voice of the divine lover has fallen silent and all they have left are his letters.

Or could it be that those who have taken over the religion won't pick up the phone when God rings because they don't want him disturbing the system they are now running by themselves? This tension is never far from the surface of organised religion, as this history will show. Israel began to consolidate itself like this after its return from exile in Babylon. Its scattered bones had come together again. There followed a two-hundred-year interlude in which it found the peace it had spent a thousand years searching for. During this time Israel was governed by empires whose leaders chose not to interfere with the religion of their subjects. It couldn't last.

In 333 BCE the Greek Emperor Alexander the Great ruled over much of the world and another cycle of change began in Israel. Alexander allowed Israel to follow its own religion and left it well alone. But when he died the parts of his empire we know today as Afghanistan, Iran, Iraq, Syria, Lebanon and Palestine were taken over by leaders whose style was different. They decided to impose their own brand of religion on their subjects, so it was only a matter of time before they clashed with Israel's fiercely jealous god. The king who started the fight was Antiochus IV. Greek by descent and frustrated in his ambition to be a bigger player in the region, he decided to pry his Jewish subjects away from their possessive god and impose on them the sophistication of Greek religion and culture.

In 167 BCE he turned the temple in Jerusalem into a shrine to the Greek god Zeus and sent enforcers throughout Israel to compel the Jews to make sacrifices to him. When one of them reached a village outside Jerusalem called Modin, he ordered the village priest, an old man called Mattathias, to conform to the king's decree and make the sacrifice or die. Mattathias responded by plunging the sacrificial knife not into the lamb prepared for the purpose but into the enforcer himself, making him the sacrifice.

He and his sons then mounted a three-year war against their bullying king. They won three battles against him and recaptured their polluted temple. On 14 December 164 BCE they started to cleanse, restore and rededicate it. It took them eight days, a period now observed by Jews as the Festival of Lights or Hanukkah. On each day during Hanukkah they light a candle on an eight-branched candelabrum (a *menorah*) to recall the restoration of the temple in Jerusalem after its desecration by Antiochus.

Antiochus died in 163 and life became easier for Israel. It maintained itself in a precarious state of independence for another hundred years until Rome took over in 63 BCE. And the end game began.

CHAPTER 11

The End

Bad things can happen to good people. The last book in the Christian Bible divided the bad things into what it called the Four Horsemen of the Apocalypse: War, Famine, Disease and Death. Those four have galloped through history since the beginning and they show no signs of slowing down. They are hard for anyone to deal with, but they present a particular problem for people of religious faith. If you don't believe in a god, if you don't believe there is any final meaning to existence, then suffering is just an unpleasant reality you have to deal with. But if you believe in a god you have hard questions to answer. Why does the god permit so much suffering in the world? And why is it that it's often the good who suffer and the bad who get away with it? All religions have their answers to these questions. In Judaism an early answer was that if Israel was suffering, it was because it was being punished for its sins.

In this chapter we'll think about the suffering of Israel as a *people* rather than that of any individual in particular; and for a very obvious reason. The One True God had called Israel to be his chosen race, his bride, his beloved. So why did it turn out to be such a costly relationship? Why did it cause them so much suffering? The prophet Ezekiel told them it was because they had failed to understand that being God's special people meant separating themselves from the ways of other nations and their gods. Instead, they had copied their ways. They'd got mixed up in their politics. They had even worshipped the true God as if he were an idol who wanted flattery and sacrifice instead of justice and holiness. That is why they had ended up as captives in Babylon. But after their release and return to Jerusalem they learned their lesson.

Home in Israel again they established themselves as a nation for whom religious purity would be the purpose and meaning of their lives. They would follow with careful attention the instructions found in the Pentateuch. Every day would be punctuated by rituals that kept God at the forefront of their consciousness. Every aspect of their lives would be marshalled to his service, from what they could eat to what they could touch and the people with whom they could associate. Israel became a theocracy, a god-state in which religion became the purpose of its whole existence. At last they had learned how to live in peace with their God and with themselves.

That peace had been shattered by Antiochus, and their suffering started all over again. But this time there was a difference. Now it was their *faithfulness* to God that was causing their misery. So the old explanation for their suffering as punishment no longer worked. A new explanation had to be found. During the persecution by Antiochus another story emerged. And it introduced an element to the religion of Judaism that was to have consequences not only for its own history, but also for the history of Christianity and Islam when they came along.

We have already seen that the prophets who had been the main players in Israel's history did not foretell the *future*; they told forth God's anger at Israel's *past*. During the struggle against King Antiochus a new character emerged, who claimed to see beyond death, beyond history itself, into the future God had in store for his suffering servants. Unlike the old prophets he did not take centre stage to announce what the voice had told him. He stayed in the shadows like a spy and put what he had heard and seen into writing. And, like a spy sending a report from enemy territory, he put his message into code so that only his side could read it. This method of passing on secret intelligence from God is called *apocalyptic,* a forbidding Greek word with a simple definition. It means to uncover what is hidden, the way a theatre curtain is pulled back to reveal what's happening on the stage. The best way to think of apocalyptic writers is as agents who are in on God's plans for his final fight-back against the enemy. And they are sent to prepare his people for the invasion.

The first apocalyptic agent called himself Daniel. And he put his message in a short book that only his Jewish readers could understand. He set it in Babylon during the time of the exile hundreds of years before, but it was actually a coded account of the persecutions of Antiochus that were happening at the time it was being written. The book consisted of six stories and a couple of dreams. The most famous story featured Daniel himself, and it was meant to assure the Jews that they would survive the fury of their persecutor.

In the story Daniel, one of the Jews exiled in Babylon, had become an official of the Persian Empire. He was admired by King Darius – the son of Cyrus, the king who had permitted the Jews to return to Judea – not only for his fidelity to his god but for his competence as an administrator. But Daniel's eminence had attracted the jealousy of other officials and they set a trap for him. They flattered King Darius by suggesting he should impose a law decreeing that throughout the empire for one month no one should be allowed to pray to any god other than Darius himself. Anyone who broke the law was to be thrown into a den of lions. Darius passed the law and the plotters rubbed their hands in glee. They knew that Daniel would go on praying to the God of Israel, come what may.

They crept up on him at home, found him at his prayers and reported him to the king. The king was upset when he realised he had fallen into their trap, but having signed the law he saw no way out of his dilemma. With a sad heart he sent Daniel into a den of lions as a punishment. But the next morning Daniel emerged undamaged by his night with the lions. Daniel's readers knew this story was not about something that had happened three hundred years ago in Babylon. It was about what was going on in Israel during their persecution by Antiochus for being faithful to God. Daniel was telling them that though they had been cast into the den of lions, if they stood fast God would save them. The book was meant to strengthen their resistance.

But that wasn't Daniel's only point. He didn't just want to comfort Israel in the midst of her suffering. He wanted to prepare her for God's final battle against her enemy. Unlike the Indian sages who saw time as an endlessly turning wheel from which the soul struggled to escape into blissful nothingness, Jewish thinkers saw time as an arrow fired by God that would end when it reached its target. And according to Daniel it was nearly there. At the end of time's flight Israel's suffering would finally be vindicated. Then the dead of the ages would rise from their graves to meet their maker and be subjected to his judgment. Here Daniel brings to Israel for the first time belief in life after death and a final reckoning when all scores would be settled according to God's law.

Until this moment in its history Israel had shown little interest in life after death. God was encountered in time but at death people's time was over and they left the scene. Departed souls then went to a shadowy underworld called *Sheol*. Sheol was a place of forgetting where not even God was remembered. Daniel's book changed all that. He told them that at the end of history God would erupt into time and 'those who sleep in the dust of the earth shall awake, some to everlasting life, and some to shame and everlasting contempt'.

The resurrection of the dead was a new idea in Judaism and it would always be controversial. A time would come when Jewish teachers would be divided into those who believed in it and those who did not. But it was an idea that would gather speed over time. Daniel did not believe in the resurrection of individuals one by one when they died, but in what is called a *general resurrection*. Everyone would sleep in their graves until God brought history to an end, when they would all rise at the same time to face their judgment. And Daniel didn't think there would be long to wait.

He had another big idea. To show them the end was near, God would send a very special secret agent called the *Messiah* to prepare them for the final assault. Messiah means 'anointed one'. In the past, when the Jews had appointed a king to lead them, they anointed his head with oil as a sign he was God's servant. Daniel was telling Israel that time and its sorrows would soon come to an end. And the sign that the end was near would be the arrival of the Messiah. But he wouldn't come from outer space. He wouldn't touch down from heaven. He would be one found living in their midst. And he would be revealed, his identity uncovered. Maybe he was already here – so keep your eyes open! In this way Daniel gave Israel hope for a time when their sufferings would be ended and God would wipe the tears from their eyes. So they started watching and waiting for the Messiah. But he never arrived. And things just got worse.   —

The persecution of Antiochus was playground stuff compared to what happened when the Romans took over Palestine in 63 BCE. A 150-year period of continuous unrest followed, punctuated by periods of open warfare, before the end finally came. And the temple in Jerusalem was again the lightning rod. The temple was more precious to the Jews than their own lives. It held their symbol for the God who had called them out of Egypt over a thousand years before. But the Jews' fierce passion for their god bewildered their new rulers, the Romans. To the Romans, gods were ten a penny. Sensible people didn't take them too seriously. What was it about this god that drove the Jews to such suicidal devotion?

According to legend, when the Roman general Pompey conquered Jerusalem in 63 BCE he decided to search for the god of the Jews in their temple. The temple was built as a series of courts of increasing sacredness. Pompey strode through them until he came to the sanctuary called the Holy of Holies. This was the most sacred part of the temple into which only the High Priest was permitted to enter. Reverently, Pompey stepped into the Holy of Holies, expecting to gaze on Israel's god. It was empty. Nothing there!

Because the Jews knew that nothing or *no thing* could represent the voice that had haunted them for centuries. The Second Commandment had gone deeply into their souls. They had erected this magnificent temple with its chiselled stones and its sequence of beautiful courts. They had loved it and would mourn its loss throughout their history. Yet at its heart was *nothing*! Pompey turned away, baffled by the riddle of a religion whose symbol for its god was an empty room.

Over the next century Roman bafflement turned to fury as they found it impossible to accommodate the ways of this stubborn people and their elusive god. So the Romans decided to finish them off completely. In the year 70 CE, under the leadership of a general called Titus, they flattened Jerusalem and destroyed the temple that had been massively enlarged and beautified since Pompey's visit 140 years before. At last it's over, thought Titus. I've destroyed them.

But they were far from destroyed. Dispersed to the corners of the earth in another long exile, the Jews had lost everything, except what mattered most to them: their God. They knew that no building of stone could contain their God. They were also suspicious of those who thought they could contain God in a building of words. As they endured this new exile and waited for their Messiah to come, they developed a tradition of disagreement with any attempt to define God in human terms.

And an important and irritating new character appeared on the scene, the heretic. Heretics are uncomfortable people who ask awkward questions and challenge majority thinking. They have a lot to teach us. And one of the most famous was found right in the middle of the Jewish Bible.

CHAPTER 12

Heretic

When American President John F. Kennedy wanted to reduce the number of nuclear bombs in the world because he believed they made it a more dangerous place, he encountered a lot of opposition. His most vocal critic was a nuclear physicist who believed that the more bombs America had the safer it would be. Asked about this, the President pointed out that anyone with complete conviction about anything, especially if that person was an expert, was bound to shake anybody who had an open mind. That, he went on, is the advantage of having a closed mind.

For the closed mind the only struggle left in life is the battle to impose its views on everyone else. The technical name for this kind of certainty is *orthodoxy*, from the Greek word meaning true or right belief. A person like President Kennedy, who opposed the orthodox view on nuclear bombs, was a *heretic* whose opinions were *heresy*, from another Greek word meaning one who opposed the party line. Orthodoxies and heresies are found everywhere in human life, but they are especially powerful in religion. And watching them at work will help us understand why religions are in constant and sometimes violent disagreement within themselves.

Yet most religions start as heresies. A prophet responds to an inner voice that challenges the current opinion, the way Abraham scorned the gods in his father's shop. What usually happens next is a split in which the heretic goes off and starts a new religion or sets up a competing branch of the old one. Sometimes heretics win the argument and their ideas become the new orthodoxy. Either the closed mind stays shut and the new inspiration goes elsewhere or it opens enough to let the new insight be absorbed.

Jews have been better at living with this process than the followers of other monotheistic religions. From the beginning argument and disagreement were central to their life. All religions argue, of course, but most of them close the debate as soon as they can and impose a line everyone has to accept or get out. They like things tidy. The Jewish religion was never really like that. It knew that nothing in religion was ever beyond dispute. It believed it was better to go on arguing than to lock their mind in an iron box and throw away the key. And at the heart of Judaism's holy book we find a heretic called Job arguing his cause against the orthodoxy of the day.

The story of Job had been around for a long time as a folk tale, but during the exile in Babylon an unknown poet got to work on it and used it as a way of exploring the problem of suffering. The Jews probably had a greater need to tackle the problem than any other race. Other nations and peoples had been erased from history by the action of great empires; but at least their sufferings had then ended. Suffering never seemed to end for the Jews. Finished as a nation in the year 70 CE and left with no place to call their own, they were delivered to a history of wandering and rejection everywhere they went. Never certain of safety anywhere for long, they kept their bags packed, ready for the next exodus, the next exile.

They had lost land and temple, but they had kept their book and it became a spiritual home for them, one they could shove in their suitcases when the next expulsion began. And even if it was taken from them they carried its essence in their memory in a few verses from the Pentateuch they all knew by heart. They called it the Shema, from the Hebrew word for *hear* or *listen*. 'Hear, O Israel: The Lord our God is one Lord; and you shall love the Lord your God with all your heart, and with all your soul, and with all your might'. According to an ancient Jewish tradition Daniel had recited the Shema in the lion's den and emerged unscathed. And the Daniel story had encouraged Israel in a moment of great peril. But what could encourage the Jewish people now that they had been ground to dust in the lions' jaws? Why was suffering now Israel's *life*?

That was the question the Book of Job responded to. Job did not have a confident answer to the question his people had been asking for centuries. What he did was destroy the orthodox view that it was God's punishment for their sins. And it is a big moment in the history of religion. It presents us with a simple man who knows a wrong idea when he sees it. Yet his religion tells him it can't be wrong because God says it's right. So he asks himself: can God make a wrong thing right just by saying it is? No, a wrong is a wrong, whatever God says or whatever the priests tell me God has said. I know their explanation is wrong and I am going to say so even if the heavens fall about me. Job is the heretic who stands up in the middle of the Bible and challenges its own teaching.

When the Book of Job opens we are told that he is a good man and righteous man who happens to be fabulously wealthy. As well as having seven sons and three daughters he adores, he possesses seven thousand sheep, three thousand camels, five hundred yoke of oxen, five hundred she-asses, and servants and estates beyond counting. In the currency of that time and place, he was rich beyond all reckoning.

But within a few days everything is taken from him. His livestock are stolen, his servants and children killed and he himself is smitten with a terrible skin disease. He is left sitting in a rubbish dump scratching himself with a piece of broken pottery. His suffering is absolute. His wife tells him he should curse God and die. But Job's response to all his suffering was to say: 'Naked I came from my mother's womb, and naked shall I return; the Lord gave, and the Lord has taken away; blessed be the name of the Lord'.

In the next scene Job is approached by three friends who say they have come to comfort him, but have actually come to interrogate him. They are the kind of believers who have an answer for everything, even the tsunami of loss that has engulfed Job. Eliphaz the Temanite, Bildad the Shuhite and Zophar the Naamathite gather in front of their stricken friend and begin their inquisition. They say the same things over and over again with increasing exasperation, but it is Eliphaz the Temanite who goes first with the official explanation for Job's condition.

The innocent never perish, says Eliphaz, while the wicked reap a harvest of pain. You are reaping a harvest of pain so tell us, what have you been up to that's brought all this misery upon your shoulders? Job refuses to accept the logic of their accusation. Whatever reason God has for his onslaught on him, it cannot be because Job's sins have brought it on his own head. Job knows he is a righteous man who has done nothing to deserve this.

Job's friends don't approach him with an open mind. It never occurs to them that the official theory might be wrong. Were they to entertain that possibility, everything in their tidy religious universe would unravel. Better to stick to the line than fall into doubt. But Job sticks to his story. The doctrine must be wrong because he knows he has done nothing to deserve the devastation that has wiped out his family and fortune.

An ordinary man thrust into an extraordinary situation, rather than submit to the accusations laid against him, Job finds the courage to challenge a brutal theory. Even if it is impossible to prove his innocence in this life – proving a negative is always impossible – he believes that after his death God will vindicate his reputation: 'For I know that my Redeemer lives, and that at the last he will stand upon the earth; and after my skin has been thus destroyed, then in my flesh I shall see God, whom I shall see on my side, and my eyes shall behold, and not another'.

But Job does not have to wait for death to get his vindication. God himself appears and denounces those who have tried to convict Job of offending him: 'The Lord said to Eliphaz the Temanite: "My wrath is kindled against you and against your two friends; for you have not spoken of me what is right, as my servant Job has". It is the heretic who gets God's blessing, not the orthodox teachers who trot out the party line.

But even God wasn't allowed to challenge the orthodox teaching in the story! A later writer, upset by God's approval of Job's heresy, stitched a happy ending onto the text. God gives Job 'twice as much as he had before', thereby reinstating the old theory that the good are rewarded and the evil punished for their deeds in this life. The genius of the story is that it lets us see heresy and orthodoxy in action. And lets us make up our own minds.

When we consider this story, it is worth going back to the Second Commandment's rejection of idols. It warned Israel against thinking it could wrap up God in neat little packages to push in the religious market place. Yet that's what organised religion usually does. It boxes God into its own orthodoxies and tries to force them on others. That's what Job's comforters had done. Rather than sitting alongside him in his despair and sharing in his bafflement at what had struck him, they told him exactly how God's hand was at work in his situation and insisted that he accepted their explanation. Highly developed religious orthodoxies love doing this. Telling people exactly what to think, explaining to them what things mean and how God fits into the situation. To be subjected to the torrent of explanation that some religions go in for is like finding yourself stuck on a long bus journey beside a compulsive talker who insists on unloading his obsessions on you all night long.

Eliphaz the Temanite, Bildad the Shuhite and Zophar the Naamathite are classic religious zealots who think they've got everything taped and love nothing more than playing the tape to anyone they meet. The great thing about the Book of Job is that it is not afraid to bore us almost to death listening to them in order to make its point. Don't be so sure you know what God is or what God's up to, is its message.

Jews have been better at living with this kind of uncertainty than most other believers. They don't try to inflict their God on other people. They're too busy arguing with him themselves to have time for that. And they are arguing still.

But we must now leave them to continue their long argument with God while we move on to consider another religion, Zoroastrianism. It will take us back to Persia at the time of the Buddha around 600 BCE. But first we'll have to make a stopover in India.

CHAPTER 13

The Last Battle

On the top of the Malabar Hills south of the city of Mumbai on the west coast of India, tourists might catch a glimpse through their binoculars of a mysterious stone tower rising above the trees. They are forbidden to climb the hill to visit the tower themselves, but if they used a drone to photograph it they would see that it has a flat roof surrounded by a low perimeter wall. And the roof is divided into three concentric circles. The camera might catch sight of carrion-eating birds at work on the roof, devouring the dead bodies that are arranged there, men on the first circle, women on the second circle and the tiny bodies of children on the third circle.

What the drone is revealing is not an act of careless indifference to the dead, but a work of profound reverence, the ancient funeral rite of the Parsees, India's smallest religious community. Parsees believe that dead bodies are unclean, so if they were to bury them they would pollute the earth that received them and if they burned them they would pollute the fire that consumed them. They also believe in being kind to the scavenging animals that help keep the earth clean, so they build these Towers of Silence on which they expose their dead to the withering heat of the sun and the sharp beaks of the crows and vultures. Once laid out on the tower it doesn't take long for the corpses to be stripped of their flesh, leaving their skeletons to bleach and disintegrate until they are gathered into the bone chamber at the centre of the tower, where they slowly return to dust and filter through the soil to be washed into the sea. So the body a human loses at death becomes the gift of continuing life to the animals who feed on it. Everything is returned to nature. Nothing is wasted.

Though the Parsees who build these Towers of Silence have been in India for many centuries, they came originally from Persia, as their name suggests. Persia was the name the Greeks gave to Iran, a land to the north-west of India. The Parsees follow a religion called Zoroastrianism that originated in Iran about the time of Israel's exile in Babylon in the sixth century BCE. Other than the Parsees in India, there aren't many Zoroastrians left in the world today, but their religion has had a profound effect on other faiths, including Judaism. And since Judaism gave birth to Christianity and Islam, two of the world's most populous religions, we could describe Zoroaster, the founder of Zoroastrianism, as one of history's most influential religious figures. It is never possible to be certain of the dates from a time when few records were kept, but it is likely that Zoroaster was born in 628 BCE and died in 551 BCE, murdered by a rival priest.

The fact that Zoroaster, a priest, was murdered by another priest reminds us again of one of religion's strongest characteristics: its capacity for violent disagreement. This is because the ultimate source of religion is a place we cannot survey in the way that the size of a remote island might be measured to settle a dispute. The source of religion is off-earth in a reality beyond this one. Its secrets are disclosed to us by prophets who claim to have penetrated its mysteries. They announce to the world what their voices have told them and a new religion is born. But since every new religion is seen as an attack on an old one, it's no surprise that the priests of the old one always gang up on the prophets of the new one. That's why one of the greatest figures in religious history said that prophets always had to suffer and die for their visions. Zoroaster was the priest of an old religion who became the prophet of a new one, so he was bound to land in trouble.

The easiest religious dispute to understand is between polytheists and monotheists, between those who believe the universe is teeming with gods and those who believe there is only one. Abraham was the first monotheist, and Zoroaster has a right to stand alongside him. But what he saw in his visions and heard in his voices was far more complicated than anything revealed to Abraham. This was because, like many religious visionaries, Zoroaster was obsessed with a problem.

Monotheism may clear away the clutter of millions of competing gods, but it comes with difficulties of its own. As we have seen, Israel's difficulty was the problem of suffering. Why did God's choice of them bring with it such constant pain and sorrow? Zoroaster's difficulty was deeper and more universal. Sufferers ask why bad things happen to good people. Zoroaster wanted to go deeper and find out how goodness and badness entered the world in the first place. For humans, life was a battle for survival not only against the elements, but against their own kind, many of whom were cruel and indifferent to the pain they inflicted on their fellows. Where did such evil come from? And will those who endure it ever be recompensed and those who inflict it ever be punished?

Those were the questions that wrenched Zoroaster out of his contented life as a priest of the old polytheistic religion of Persia. Like many spiritual searchers before him, they prompted him to spend years in solitary meditation pondering the nature of evil. Then the solution came to him. In a series of visions it was revealed to him that the struggle between good and evil was older than human history. It had its origin in the very heart of God! There was indeed one supreme God, whom he called the Wise Lord or Ahura Mazda, but he discovered complexity within the life of the one God. In the beginning the Wise Lord had fathered non-identical twins, allowing each of them to choose his own path. One chose goodness. The other chose evil. One chose the truth. The other chose the lie.

So the world – and each individual within it – became the arena for a dramatic battle between good and evil in which the sons fought with each other and tried to win us to their side. Like the sons of the Wise Lord, we too have to decide whose side we are on.

Zoroaster's pushing of the struggle between good and evil back into the life of God did not really solve the problem he struggled with. A full explanation would have required the Wise Lord to say why he chose to create evil in the first place and put his children at its mercy. But what Zoroaster did with great power was to dramatise the situation in which we all find ourselves. Like a brilliant novelist, he described human life as a series of battles. And our moral struggles do lend themselves to the language of warfare. We *fight* our addictions. We *struggle* against temptations. Even the idea of an actual spirit of evil can make sense. There are ideas that can infect the human mind like a virus and prompt it to terrible actions. Racism is the most obvious example but there are many others.

But Zoroaster was more than a dramatist who held a mirror up to human experience. Like Daniel he was an apocalyptic who saw beyond history to the time when God would bring the world's story to a conclusion. Good books need a final chapter in which loose ends are tied together and a satisfying resolution is achieved. This urge is strong in religions that see history as an arrow, not a circle: a story with a beginning, middle and end, not a wheel that endlessly turns.

Zoroaster did not believe that good and evil would forever be caught in a standoff. There would be a final reckoning. The Wise Lord's creation of good and evil was designed to give us the freedom to choose our own destiny and the time to get it right. And he wasn't indifferent to our choices. The tragedy of those who chose evil was that they had not looked far enough ahead to see the consequences of their actions. Each choice helped to form their character and at the end they would be judged on the kind of person they had made themselves. At death each soul crossed the Chinvat Bridge or Bridge of Reckoning into the destiny it had prepared for itself. The bridge was as narrow as a razor. On its far side lay Paradise, but underneath it lay Hell. What happened was that the soul had either made itself so heavy with evil that its weight pulled it off the bridge into Hell or so light with good that it easily danced across into Paradise.

Even that was not the most dramatic element in Zoroaster's vision of the end. The problem of the existence of evil itself had to be resolved, the very evil that pulled souls off the bridge to Paradise. Zoroaster's solution came at what he called the 'last turn of creation', when the Wise Lord would finally destroy the wicked twin, the principle of evil. The world would be renewed and goodness and justice would finally prevail. And a saviour, called a *saoshyant* or one who brings benefit, would appear. Through his agency evil would be finally defeated and the renewal of the world would follow.

As well as being vivid and scary, Zoroaster's teaching was hugely influential. And it brought a number of new themes into world religion. It is where we first find the idea of individual resurrection either to the joy of Paradise or the torment of Hell. And it is where we first discover the idea of a great battle at the end of time into which God sends a saviour to destroy evil and establish a world of righteousness and justice. We have already noticed how Daniel brought these same ideas to bear in his attempts to console suffering Israel, ideas that may have been picked up by the Jews during their exile in Persia. It reminds us that religions are not sealed off from each other and that a lot of cross-fertilisation goes on.

Zoroaster met opposition but he also met with approval and success. His teachings were gathered into sacred scriptures called the *Avesta*. And the process that transforms heresy into orthodoxy began. The Zoroastrians always mistrusted imagery, but they did have their own symbol for the Wise Lord – fire. They kept a sacred fire lit in their temples, which is why they have been wrongly described as fire worshippers. Fire was certainly sacred to them, but only as a symbol for the eternal life of the Wise Lord.

They advised their followers that the practice of good thoughts, good words and good deeds while they lived would help speed their souls across the Chinvat Bridge when they were dead and their corpses had been spread on the roof of the Towers of Silence as a gift to the birds of the air. Towers of Silence can still be found on Iranian hilltops, memorials from the past to what was once the country's main religion. But Zoroastrianism suffered from the same law that saw it replace a previous creed, and in time its end drew near. It endured for centuries in Iran, the land of its birth, but 1,300 years ago it was replaced by an assertive new religion called Islam. It was at this time that Zoroastrians made the long journey to India where they were free once more to light their sacred fire, build their Towers of Silence, think good thoughts, speak good words and perform good deeds. And there, though few in numbers, they remain.

Before starting a new chapter I want to look back at some of the ground we've covered to draw some conclusions from what we have learned. A good place to start is with the Jains' parable of the blind men and the elephant. Its message was that because of their limited vision humans were incapable of achieving perfect knowledge of ultimate reality, so they should be modest about the religious claims they make.

In spite of that warning, the prophets and sages of religion are rarely in doubt about their beliefs, because they have 'seen' and 'heard' what lies behind the veil that hangs between humans and ultimate reality. I have inserted cautious inverted commas round the verbs *seen* and *heard* to remind us that we have to decide for ourselves how to respond to the claims they made about their experiences. Because they all saw different things or saw the same things differently!

Hindu sages saw the turning of the wheel of karma and rebirth and the endless circling of time itself. And these ideas became the central doctrines of Indian religion.

Jewish prophets saw the One True God who, when the time was ripe, would send his messiah to bring history to a close, the hope that sustains many believing Jews to this day.

Zarathustra saw a final conflict between good and evil at the end of time, in which good would triumph.

Though each interpreted it differently, the founders of these religions were more interested in what they saw on the other side of history than in what happened here.

But when we get to China on our next stop we'll discover that its sages were more interested in how best to live in this life than in what awaited them in the next. So let us now head east along one of the oldest and longest trade routes in the world – the Silk Road – to find out more. It will carry us all the way to China and an interesting take on life called Confucianism.

CHAPTER 14

Worldly Religion

The Silk Road ran along the northern border of India into China and began its life around 206 BCE, when a Chinese emperor sent merchants west to sell to the peoples of India his country's most important export, silk. In time the Silk Road extended its reach for four thousand miles to the shores of the Mediterranean on the edge of Europe. Caravans of riders on horseback made their way along the route, bringing silk and other goods to the west and returning east with wool and textiles. But it wasn't just silk and other goods that were carried along this famous road. Ideas were exchanged and religions were imported as well. Buddhism was brought into China by traders from India and established itself as one of the three main Chinese religions.

But China had its own approach to religion and the best word to describe it is *pragmatic*, another Greek word with a straightforward meaning. It comes from a word meaning act or deed, from which the English word 'practical' comes. It meant practice as opposed to theory, right-doing rather than right-believing.

Even early Chinese polytheism was practical and matter-of-fact. China's gods were representations of the forces of nature or the vagaries of the weather. And in their ceremonies the Chinese called upon their gods to bless them with favourable conditions and drive away anything that might harm them. Their top god, the God of Gods in Heaven, sent the rain that watered the crop fields that sustained them in life. But where there is rain there are floods. The god responsible for floods was Gong Gong. And where there are floods there are sometimes droughts. Ba was the goddess of drought. And what was more important to humans than the food that sustained them? The millet god, Hou Ji, celebrated the importance of the cereal-bearing grasses that grew in their fields.

Keeping all these forces in balance made sense. It was the practical thing to do. Religion wasn't about believing things, it was about doing things. It was the sensible way to manage the forces of nature in order to provide good things for the human community.

As well as trying to manage the gods of nature, the Chinese had a gallery of mischievous spirits they tried to avoid: demons, pixies, vampires, gnomes, goblins and dragons. To scare them off they invented fireworks, and to this day the Chinese love spectacular pyrotechnical displays.

The Chinese may have had their own practical way of responding to these supernatural forces but there was little that was original in their polytheism. Their gods were the common imaginings of the human race's deep past, dreamed up by minds that gazed in wonder at the universe they found themselves in. It is when we come to the fifth and sixth centuries BCE that we see China's pragmatic approach to life achieving new clarity and direction. Around the time that Buddhists and Jains were reacting against the religion of India and Jewish exiles were rethinking the nature of their God in Babylon, we find a different mood among China's thinkers. It is to *this* world that the Chinese sages apply their creative minds, not the after-world, the world to come. And the most significant of them was the man we call Confucius.

The name Confucius is our version of Kong Fuzi or Kong the Master or Philosopher, the name given to Kong Qiu, a thoughtful official of one of the states into which China was divided at the time. We possess the barest outline of his life, but in his writings we meet a wise and generous mind that had its greatest impact long after his death. He was born in 551 BCE during a time of chaos in China, when the leaders of rival states were engaged in constant warfare with each other. Just as the politicians and thinkers of the twenty-first century struggle to find answers to the problems that beset humanity today, so did the sages of their time offer solutions to China's difficulties. And the solutions suggested were not unlike what we hear from our politicians today. Fight violence with violence, fire with fire. Hit the enemy harder than they hit us. Make bigger guns and more lethal bombs. And find tougher leaders to take on the bad guys. Throughout history, political strategies have usually read like the script of the latest Hollywood blockbuster.

Confucius' line was different. He told the warlords that the welfare of the people should be their aim and object. To achieve it they should choose ministers who were trained in ethics and were skilled in handling human disagreement without turning to violence. The leaders listened and bowed to Confucius' wisdom, murmuring approvingly. But none was prepared to put his ideas into practice. Confucius had patience as well as wisdom. He spent the rest of his life explaining his ideas to his disciples, hoping that one day an enlightened ruler would put them into practice. He died in 479 BCE, but because his disciples had recorded his teaching in books his ideas lived on. Their time would come. Around 100 BCE an emperor emerged who put his ideas into practice and they became the dominant philosophy of China until the imperial system was overthrown in 1912. And even in the Communist China of today Confucian principles still have a hold.

Confucius' main idea is the opposite of rugged individualism or the cult of loners who pit themselves against society and its restrictions. From the moment of our birth we are held in a web of relationships, Confucius taught, and we could not survive without it. What is good for the community is good for the individual, even if it sometimes means the denial of the individual's private wishes. Life is relational. Society is a body of which we are all members. Individual limbs cannot survive if they separate themselves from it. And compassion is the glue that holds it all together. Compassion means *suffering together*. Compassionate people try to feel their way into the experience of others to see things from their angle. It is from Confucius that we get one of the earliest expressions of what is known as the Golden Rule. It comes in both a positive and a negative form: 'Do to others as you would like them to do to you'. Or: 'Do not do to others what you would not like them to do to you'.

The word Confucius used to capture this spirit of understanding and sympathy towards others was *ren*. In keeping with the Chinese principle of pragmatism *ren* is better seen in action than understood in theory. If you sacrifice your life to save another's, you are practising *ren*. If I am on my way to the store to buy a gadget I have saved for months to acquire and I give my money instead to a homeless refugee, I am practising *ren*. *Ren* is the noblest behaviour a human being is capable of. It is to put others before oneself. And it was the spirit Confucius wanted to find in politicians and leaders. He wanted them to concentrate on the well-being of their people, not on their own ambitions. And he hoped ordinary citizens would follow the same spirit of generosity in how they judged the leaders who were struggling to govern well in difficult times.

The Confucian approach to managing human disagreement and conflict teaches patience and consideration of others as well as compassion. This is why, in practice, it is associated with an almost stylised courtesy. Courtesy and patience are the marks of a mind aware of the complexity of human relationships and the care required to conduct them. To this day courtesy in the interactions between people seems to be more present in the patient eastern mind than in the hasty western mind.

But isn't Confucianism better understood as a philosophy rather than as a religion? Defining the difference between these terms will help us decide the issue. *Philosophy*, another useful Greek word, means love of wisdom in all its forms. And the form known as moral philosophy is the study of the best or wisest way to live in this world. Whereas religion is more interested in what lies beyond this world *over there*. And what it will be like for us when our life has ended.

These are not the questions that interest Confucianism. It concentrates its energies on managing life on earth for the good of the human community, not on earning merits or avoiding penalties in the life to come. Life is to be lived well for its own sake and not just as a prelude to what may happen to us after death.

However, there is a side to Confucianism that brings it into the religious sphere: its approach to death and its veneration of ancestors. But this can also be understood as an extension of the philosophy that sees humans as bonded together in society. Not even death can sever the bonds between us. That is why in Confucian societies the dead are mourned intensely and their memory is cherished constantly. The periods of mourning after a death vary, but for children of the deceased it can be more than two years, during which they would not work, have sex, eat any but the simplest food, wear nice clothes or generally enjoy themselves.

But for Confucius there was more to the veneration of ancestors than mourning their loss. The dead had not ceased to exist. Nor had we lost contact with them. They may have left the scene here and gone to the place beyond, but they retained a continuing presence in our lives. Because they were out of sight did not mean they were out of mind. That's why a favourite Confucian spring holiday was the Clear and Bright festival, when families visited the graves of their ancestors to commune with them and enjoy each other again. Courtesy and respect for all – even if they happened to be dead – was the hallmark of Confucianism.

But it never had it all its own way in China. It was one of three almost interchangeable approaches to life. The other two were Taoism and Buddhism. In the next chapter we'll examine Taoism and take another look at Buddhism to find out what happened to it when it finally reached China in the first century CE.

CHAPTER 15

The Way to Go

Confucianism may be easy to understand but it's a serious business. It's not much fun. With Taoism, another Chinese tradition,
it's the other way round. Taoism is hard to get your head round but,
once you get the hang of it, it can be fun. Like the sages of other
religions, the originators of Taoism discovered something, but it's
where they found it that made them different. The Hindu sages
saw that the world and our lives within it were illusions that had to
be dispelled if we were to achieve salvation. The Jewish prophets
saw that God intended to bring the world to an end one day and
judge what its inhabitants had done during the time of its existence. For both these religions the world and the place of humans
within it were problems that had to be resolved. And they went
outside to find the answers.

Taoists were different. It was the world they looked at. And they
loved what they saw. They were moved by its unity and interde-
pendence, the way it held together. Except for the human side of it!
Humans were out of sync with the universe because their self-
conscious minds had divorced them from its natural rhythms.

Peace lay in recovering harmony with nature and living according to its beat. It was how they expressed this that made it hard for some to follow. They invited humans to live according to the *Tao* of the universe, but they did not explain what the Tao was. It got even harder when they told people they couldn't learn the Tao unless they already knew the Tao. And harder still when they said those who knew the Tao didn't talk about it and those who talked about it didn't know it. Reading this, you are probably racking your brain to figure out what Tao is. Like any rational person, you want things explained. You want to understand what's going on. Your mind demands it. The Taoist only increases your irritation by smiling kindly at you and saying nothing!

So it's worth recalling times in your life when working grimly at something made it impossible. But when you gave up struggling it happened. A good example is the moment in the swimming pool you started swimming for the first time. Or the summer afternoon you found your balance and realised you were actually riding your bike along the street. *Balance* is the key. Only those who already have it know what it is. We might call it the Tao of cycling. Taoism wants us to find that same balance in how we live and relate, not only to other people but to the whole universe.

The man behind this approach to life was an older contemporary of Confucius called Laozi or Lao Tse. Born around 600 BCE, he is said to have worked in the library of one of the Chinese emperors. When asked to explain his approach to life he produced one of the shortest and most revered texts in the history of religion or philosophy, called the *Lao Tzu* or 'Book of the Way'. Its most important ideas were 'balance' and 'complementarity'. Lao Tse saw that in nature everything had its complementary opposite. He called these opposites Yang and Yin. Every Yin had its Yang, every Yang its Yin. To make the distinction clear, Taoists drew a circle divided by a curve into two equal parts, one white and the other black. And each distinctive half contained a dot of its opposite, a black dot in the white half and a white dot in the black half. It advises us to find ourselves in the other: the white in the black, the black in the white; the feminine in the masculine, the masculine in the feminine; the friend in the enemy, the enemy in the friend; my religion in yours and yours in mine. It's not unlike Confucius telling us to imagine ourselves in the place of the other. But Lao Tse puts a joyful spin to it. He doesn't want us to *tolerate* diversity. He wants us to *revel* in it. The world is an orchestra of hundreds of different instruments working together to make beautiful music. Balance, timing and harmony: these are the marks of the Tao.

Lao Tse noticed that another way humans lose balance is in their need to control others. Rather than letting them live by their own rhythm, they constantly interfere with them. The supreme example is the person for whom their way is the only way to do anything, from loading the dishwasher to running the country. People like this are in a state of constant irritation because reality won't comply with the pattern they want to impose on it. Lao Tse told them to relax and learn from the life of a plant. It doesn't have to be told how to do its thing. It follows its nature. Why can't humans do the same? Why can't they stop agitating, and let things flow? Lao Tse called his approach to life *wu-wei*, doing-by-not-doing, letting things be, letting things happen. He disliked rules and regulations and the way compulsive organisers crowd everyone onto their spot in the circle of life instead of celebrating their differences.

The term for someone who adopts this approach to life is an *anarchist*, another Greek word meaning one who is against the government. For the Taoist it's not about absolute opposition to government, it's about wanting balance and proportion in government. It is about being wary of the dominant role of law-makers in society and disliking the way they try to force everyone into the same mould. The opposite of an anarchist is a *legalist*, someone who believes law is the only way to control human nature. Something's become a problem for society? Ban it! Forbid it! That's always the cry of the legalist.

Unlike Confucius, who wants to control human nature for the good of society as a whole, Lao Tse wants to give the individual as much freedom as possible within society. Rival approaches to life, the Yin and Yang again, each with something to be said for it. But because they are history's great organisers and rarely take a day off, legalists usually get the upper hand in religion and society and set about imposing their will on others. And if they have to, they'll even wage war to get their own way. Lao Tse hated war, the destroyer of human harmony. Maybe if people had listened to him there would have been more fun and less war in the world.

You can learn a lot from Taoism without accepting its explicitly religious ideas, but it would be wrong for us to ignore their existence. Taoism continued to develop after Lao Tse died in 524 BCE. And as well as teaching the Tao it had many gods. Its supreme deities, known as the Celestial Worthies, were believed to have been spontaneously created when the world came into existence. These top gods held court in heaven, supported by a household staff of lesser gods. As well as the gods that came with the universe, humans themselves could become gods or *immortals*. To achieve immortal status they had to purge their imperfections through a regime of meditation and suppression of desire like the Buddha's programme for achieving release from the wheel of rebirth. The difference was that Taoists believed in the universe. For them, the triumph of the soul was not to disappear like a raindrop into the ocean of nirvāna but to achieve personal immortality as a god. Another characteristic that distinguished Taoism from other religions was the place it gave to women. As well as female gods, Taoism had women priests and scholars who played an important part in its history. True to its own philosophy, Taoism lived by the feminine principle Yin as well as the masculine principle Yang.

Confucianism and Taoism were native to China, but its third religion, Buddhism, was an import from India. After Buddha's moment of enlightenment under the wild fig tree, his teaching spread throughout India, Southeast Asia, China, Korea, Japan and beyond. As it grew, it divided into different denominations based on rival interpretations of the Buddha's words. *Theravada Buddhism* remained true to the strictness of the original movement. For it, the quickest route to salvation was to become a monk. This is known as 'Small Vehicle Buddhism'. It's a racing car to enlightenment for the gifted individual. *Mahayana*, or 'Great Vehicle Buddhism,' was a bus for ordinary people who had to take their time.

Speed was not the only difference between them. We have already noticed the great division in religion between those who love images and those who hate them. The Buddha rejected them, but popular religion likes something to look at and what better image could there be for Buddhists to venerate than the Buddha himself? Statues of the Buddha, often astonishingly beautiful, became the dominant object in Buddhist temples in the Mahayana tradition. It was this form of Buddhism that came along the Silk Road into China in the first and second centuries CE. It took root and changed Chinese religion. And was changed by it.

The Chinese continued to be pragmatic in their approach to religion. They didn't mind mixing the best bits of different traditions, nor were they hung up on strict adherence to a single faith. So when Buddhism met Taoism, both were changed by the encounter. One result was *Zen Buddhism*, from the Chinese word for meditation. Remember how hard it was to *get* the Tao? Zen borrowed its teasing approach.

How can I find peace and stop all this craving? Teach me. Tell me how the holy books explain my situation and how to escape from it.

Out . . . in . . . out . . . in.

What?

Sit still, very still . . . count your breaths: out . . . in . . . out . . . in.

I come to you with my problems and you give me a breathing exercise! I need something else, something I can get my mind round.

OK. Take a long look at this daisy . . .

WHAT?

Zen has the playfulness of Taoism, and cultures dominated by rationality can learn a lot from it.

A third denomination that emerged in Buddhism had a profound effect on one of the most mysterious countries on earth. *Tantric Buddhism* offered the intensive help of a teacher in the pursuit of enlightenment, and it was this form of Buddhism that rooted itself in Tibet. Found on the other side of the Himalayas, south-west of China, Tibet is one of the most inaccessible regions on earth. It is called the Roof of the World because it is composed of huge mountains and immense plateaux. Its remoteness encouraged a form of Buddhism that turned the whole country into a vast monastery. Under the leadership of teaching monks called lamas, Tibet became a nation centred on the disciplines of Buddhist spirituality.

And the Tibetan lamas made distinctive use of one of Buddhism's traditions. When a monk achieved enlightenment he could renounce his ticket to nirvāna and volunteer to come back to earth as a 'living Buddha' to help others find salvation. In the Tibetan tradition some of the high lamas were allowed to choose their own reincarnations, but the one they had chosen as successor had to be searched for. On the lama's death the hunt for his replacement could take several years. When identified after passing a number of tests, he was proclaimed the lama's reincarnation and installed in one of the monasteries. The best-known of these lines of succession today is that of the Dalai Lama, whose smiling face has become familiar in the West since his escape from Tibet after China's invasion in the 1950s. He is the thirteenth reincarnation of the first Dalai Lama and may well be the last. This does not mean that Buddhism's day is over in Tibet. Religion has a way of outliving its persecutors. It is an anvil that has worn out many hammers. But Buddhism did not stop when it reached China. It kept on moving east until it reached Japan where it encountered our next religion, Shinto.

CHAPTER 16

Stirring up the Mud

When talking about Tibet in the previous chapter I described it as remote and inaccessible. I was speaking carelessly. The parable of the blind men and the elephant warned us against assuming that the world is how we see it. To me Tibet is remote. To a Tibetan it is home and Scotland is remote. I was about to make the same mistake about Japan. It was over the sea and far away from China. Even the Chinese, their nearest neighbours, didn't visit it until 600 CE. So it was tempting to think of Japan as cut off from the rest of the world. But why not think of the world as cut off from Japan? For a long time the people of Japan didn't know there was a world to be cut off from. They thought Japan was the world. And not only was Japan their world. Japan was their religion, they loved it so much! So to understand the religion of Japan we have to try to understand how the Japanese felt about their land.

The word *Japan* is itself a giveaway. It was a European attempt at pronouncing the Chinese word for the country. The natives called it Nippon or Land of the Rising Sun, a description that fitted. Looking east, all they saw was the glittering emptiness of the

Pacific Ocean, out of which the sun rose every day to pour itself upon the 6,852 islands of the Japanese archipelago. So it is no surprise that in the Nipponese creation story the sun played a big part. All religions have creation stories, giving their versions of how the world came to be. It is time to look at a few of them and draw some conclusions before coming back to Japan.

India had many creation stories. One of them claimed that before time existed and the world was formed, there was a huge being called Purusha who exploded and from his scattered elements everything came into being, down to the fine detail of the Hindu caste system.

The people of Mesopotamia, the birthplace of Abraham, said that in the beginning there were two giants, Apsu, or Sweet Water, and Tiamat, or Salt Water. They mated together and gave birth to other gods and sea monsters. And as the sea sometimes floods dry land, so the female partner Tiamat wanted to take control of everything. She was opposed and defeated by her own family. They split her corpse into heaven and earth. Heaven was fixed up for the gods. To serve them humans were invented and established in the servants' quarters down below on earth.

Egypt had similar stories, with water again as the big player. In the beginning there was only the sea. Then, as if a flood were retreating, a hill rose above the surface. In one account the sun god Ra came on the scene to create other gods and establish the earth. In another version it was the earth god Ptah who appeared first and got everything rolling.

If we head north to Scandinavia we find the same watery theme. In the beginning there was an abyss of nothingness. It filled with water. Then the water froze. Then it started to melt. From the melting water a giant called Ymir appeared. Out of his armpits a man and a woman then emerged. While all this was going on, a cow licked the ice thin enough to let another giant burst out. From this giant the god Odin descended. As usually happened in the careers of these gods, all hell then broke loose. Odin and his brothers killed Ymir and from his body they made the earth, from his skull they made the heavens and from his blood the sea. His bones became mountains and trees flowed from his hair. There are other details, but you get the picture.

After all this mayhem it's a relief to turn to the creation story in the Jewish Bible, dating from around 900 BCE. There are two versions in Genesis, each resolutely monotheistic, and in each the sea features. It is 'the deep' that God broods over and from which he calls everything into being. He does the job in six days and rests on the seventh. Doing nothing on the seventh day was itself a creative act that established the Sabbath as a day off for everyone.

The Japanese story comes from about the same time as Genesis, and the sea is again a big player. In the beginning there was only the sea. Then the god Izanagi and the goddess Izanami used a long spear to stir up the mud at the bottom of the sea and from the mud the many islands of Japan were formed. The divine couple then gave birth to three children, the Sun Goddess and her brothers the Moon God and the Storm God. The Sun Goddess had children of her own and her grandson became the first emperor of Nippon.

It's worth thinking about these stories for a moment because they tell us much about how religion works. Are they true or false? That depends on what you think their purpose is. Do you remember the story the prophet Nathan told King David? Was that true or false? Factually it was false. There was no rich man who had stolen a poor man's lamb. But morally it was true. It was invented to make David think about what he had done. And it worked. It had the truth of art, not the truth of science. Science is interested in facts, the way things work. Art is interested in revealing to us the truth of our own lives. That's why a story can make you cry out in recognition: that's me! Religion is an art, not a science. So the question to ask of a creation story is not whether it is true or false, but what it means, what it's trying to tell us – a distinction many religious people never got hold of. And as we'll see, some of them make themselves look silly trying to prove that the creation story in the Bible is a work of science and not a work of art.

None of the creation stories we have looked at is factually true, but they all carry a meaning of some sort. The Bible's is the easiest to grasp, even if you don't agree with it: the universe did not create itself; it was made by God. And the Mesopotamian and Scandinavian stories of original conflict reflect the world's continuing violence and cruelty.

These stories came from the human mind. The question is whether they were put there by God or were completely invented by us. However you answer that question, the stories are interesting in themselves. And there are bits of them that might have been carried as memories from a long time ago: an explosion that began every change and an ocean that gave birth to every creature. Modern science's creation story traces the beginning of the universe to the Big Bang about fourteen billion years ago. And its best guess about how life began on our planet is that it kicked off about three and a half billion years ago. The seas that covered the young earth were a soup of chemicals from exploding volcanoes and it was from their interactions that the first life forms emerged. Billions of years later we lumbered onto the scene. Did earth's memories of its own history seep into the minds of those artists who peered through time to find the meaning of things? It doesn't seem impossible to me. That may be because the whole universe seems pretty weird and almost anything is imaginable.

The endearing thing about the Nipponese creation story is that when the gods stirred up the mud at the bottom of the ocean they did not make a world, they made Japan! Or they made a world that consisted only of Japan. It was how they explained the love they felt for their beautiful islands. Island nations can't help turning in on themselves. They are less open to the traffic that flows over land borders so their religious impulses are rarely influenced by the gods of neighbouring countries. What we know of early Japanese religion confirms that. And if we remember that Japan was never conquered until 1945 at the end of the Second World War, we will not be surprised to discover that not only did the Japanese love their island nation with a passionate love, they believed it was unique. In the very distant past they probably thought nothing else existed.

Not only was Japan created by the gods, it was their chosen abode, their dwelling-place. Other religions believed that though gods could *visit* the earth, their main residence was far above us in a special domain called heaven. For the Japanese their beautiful island nation was that special domain. Heaven and earth were one. Heaven was on earth, earth was in heaven. Some religions saw a human body as the physical dwelling place of an immortal soul. That's how the Japanese thought of their land. Japan's islands were the material expression of sacred spirits called *kami* who were everywhere in nature. They dwelt in animals. They inhabited Japan's mountains, the most beautiful and sacred being Mount Fuji. They were found in plants and rivers.

I've said this was their religion, but that's not quite correct. It suggests something separate, a belief they held in their heads. It would be just as wrong to describe your sense of yourself as a religion, something you *held* or *believed* about yourself, rather than who you *were*. The Japanese experienced themselves as enfolded in a great web of being, consisting of the land, themselves and the spirits that animated everything. It wasn't something they *believed*. It was just the way they were.

The technical name for this attitude to life is *animism*. And it is not far from a modern theory called *Gaia* that sees the planet not as something to be plundered and exploited by us, but as a living organism to be cared for with the same affection we bring to our family and friends. It means that nature is as alive with spirit and significance as human beings are. The Japanese felt this in their hearts. They were not told they *had* to love in this way as a religious imperative. They were not told they had to *believe* the world was like this. They did not observe special days that celebrated their discovery of the earth's nature. They had no *beliefs* about it. Just a love for the spirit of the land, expressed by the shrines they erected in beautiful places, each shrine marked by a distinctive gate made of two uprights and two crossbars. There are more than one hundred thousand of these shrines in Japan today and they are still cherished.

Their way of responding to the world didn't even have a name until the Chinese came to Japan around 600. The Chinese didn't come as conquerors or evangelists, but they did bring Confucianism, Taoism and Buddhism with them, and they all became established in Japan. Maybe it was because the Chinese liked to classify the beliefs and practices they came across. Or maybe the Japanese decided they needed a name that captured the love they felt for their spirit-filled land in order to distinguish it from the new religions that had established themselves in their midst. So they called it *Shinto, shin* meaning gods and *to* from the Taoist term for path or way. The Tao of Shin. The way of the gods, Shinto. The word 'love' would have done just as well.

You don't have to believe the gods created the islands of Nippon out of primeval mud to admire Shinto. It looks through the world to something deeper. Sometimes it expresses what it sees in delicately haunting paintings. Usually all it needs to celebrate its love of the world are the three lines of a poem called a haiku.

A summer river being crossed
how pleasing
with sandals in my hands!

CHAPTER 17

Religion Gets Personal

Religion has served many purposes in human history. Before modern science gave its account of the creation, religious visionaries offered their descriptions, some of which we've just dipped into. But as well as trying to describe *how* the world was created, religion also tried to explain *why* it was organised the way it was. If asked why humans were the dominant species on the planet and did what they liked with it, the Bible told them it was because God had arranged it that way. God had put us in charge of the earth and told us to conquer and control it. When asked why humanity was divided into groups graded according to the colour of their skin, the Hindu scriptures replied that things had been ordered that way by the intelligence behind the universe for a purpose. It was karma.

These responses didn't just say that's the way things are, get used to it. They gave the stamp of divine approval to the way the world was organised. It was how God had planned it. That's why religion has been so good at persuading people to accept their lot in life no matter how miserable, especially since it also offers them the hope of something better in the next one or next time round in this one.

And religion is also good at getting people to accept the rules and regulations imposed on them by society. If you want humans to live in harmony with each other they'll need an agreed set of customs – a *morality*. Don't tell lies. Don't steal. Don't kill. Any intelligent community would protect itself with prohibitions like these. What religion does is to add weight to the rules by saying they were not a human invention, they were a divine command. It wasn't the Israelites in the wilderness who dreamt up the Ten Commandments. They were imposed on them by God. So another of religion's big roles in history has been as the guardian of morality.

Now we must look at a development that took religion in a more private direction. As well as being a group activity, a way of controlling the human *community*, religion started offering *individuals* personal salvation. The word *salvation* comes from the Latin for health, a reminder that humans are often sick and anxious. They don't feel well or happy or at ease with themselves in this life. And they worry about what awaits them in the next. When religion took a turn in a more personal direction, it was able to bring such peace into troubled lives that believers described the experience as dying and being born again, or being blind and seeing again, or being paralysed and walking again. It seems to have been the meeting of different religions with each other for the first time that prompted this development.

And unlikely as it may seem, it was Roman soldiers who gave it its biggest shove. By 30 BCE the Romans had overwhelmed the Persian and Greek empires. Politically the Romans were the victors, but they soaked up so much of the culture of the countries they'd taken over that in the end it was sometimes hard to say who the real winners were. The Romans were so taken with the myths they discovered among their Greek and Persian subjects that they adopted them in a way that had a significant effect on the future of religion.

Just as the Chinese had adapted Buddhism to their own way of doing things, so did the Romans with the Greek myths. The Romans were practical people, men of action. So they took these old myths and turned them into what we would now call role play. And by acting the parts in the stories, their own lives were changed. It wasn't a case of believing the myths they'd picked up from Greek religion. It was turning them into emotional or psychological experiences that mattered to them.

But it's a mistake to think the Greeks *had* a religion the way the Jews had Judaism or the Persians had Zoroastrianism. They were more like the Japanese with their Shinto than either of the others. They were polytheists, certainly, but their gods were as much part of the landscape as their mountains and seas and the sun that shone on them. The gods did their thing much the way the weather did its thing. And like the weather the gods could be benign or threatening. That was just the way they were. There was a top god called Zeus, god of the sky, who had two brothers, Poseidon, god of the sea, and Hades, god of the underworld, the place of the dead. There were hundreds of other gods, some of them associated with the rhythms of nature. But one of the stories from their enormous library of divine adventures became the basis for an important cult in the Roman Empire that had far-reaching influence.

The story started as a nature myth, but when the Romans got hold of it they turned it into what we call a 'mystery religion', a set of secret rites and practices that provoked deep emotional experiences in its followers. In the Greek story Hades, the god of the underworld, was desperate for a wife with whom to share his gloomy estate. So he abducted Persephone, daughter of Demeter, goddess of fruit, crops and vegetation. Demeter was so devastated by the loss of her daughter that she went into deep mourning and neglected her duties. As a result, crops failed, fruit vanished from the trees and humanity was threatened with famine and death. To save the situation, Zeus intervened and worked out a deal that gave each side in the dispute half of what they wanted. Persephone was sentenced to spend half the year on earth and half the year in the underworld with her boring husband. When summer was over and she descended to Hades to do her time there, her mother Demeter would again mourn her absence. Winter struck the earth and all growing things died. Leaves fell. Trees became bare, fields barren.

But in the spring when Persephone ascended to the earth again, her mother rejoiced at her return and everything came back to life.

This is a beautiful example of how a myth crafted to account for the workings of nature can also be used to express the ups and downs of a human life. Human existence also has its rhythms of loss and recovery, failure and success, death and rebirth. The idea of a dying and rising god came to fit a deep need in the human soul. This story and the rituals designed to bring out its meaning became one of the most important mystery religions in the Roman Empire. *Mystery* comes from the Greek to be silent or keep your lips closed, because the members of the cult were sworn to secrecy about the rites and ceremonies they went through.

The cult originated in Eleusis near Athens about 1400 BCE as a holiday celebrating the goddess Demeter's gift of the fruits of the earth. But in its ritualised form in the Roman Empire, where it was known as the Eleusinian cult, the emphasis was on the spiritual experience of the *individual* who was being taken into the mystery of the god's dying and rising again. The person being admitted to the cult had communion with the goddess and experienced the winter of her dying and the spring of her rising again. This was achieved through ceremonies that copied the experience of going down into a place of darkness before being brought back into the daylight of new life. The appeal of the rituals was to the emotions. It was not something they *learned*. It was something they *felt*. And it changed them as they went through it. Remember: all of this was going on in the human mind. And we know what a strange place the mind is. It contains heaven and hell, height and depth, darkness and light. The priests of the Eleusinian cult were experts on the human mind. They knew how to lead their followers along its turns and twists up into the sunlit meadow of salvation.

But it wasn't just Greek gods like Demeter and Persephone who found new careers in the mystery religions of the Roman Empire. An old Zoroastrian god from Persia called Mithras became the centre of another Roman cult. Born in a cave, Mithras was a sun god who killed a sacred bull from whose blood the earth and its creatures were formed. Roman soldiers came across the Mithras story in their military adventures in the east. They liked its blood and sword theme. They admired the courage it took to slaughter a bull single-handed. And they liked the idea that the killing and shedding of blood they were so good at could lead to the emergence of a new and better kind of life for others. So they adopted the myth for their own purposes and it became their favourite mystery cult.

Mithraism was a bloodier affair than the Eleusinian cult, but its themes were not that different. It too celebrated a death as the gateway to new life. Its rites were also held underground and they carried a powerful emotional charge. They too were *felt* and not *learned*. Caves and caverns were spooky places anyway, so being led down into one would have had a disturbing effect on followers of the cult. A Roman soldier faced death every day, so a cult that dramatised a sacrificial death and the life that flowed from it would have been compelling for him. Mithraism was a men-only affair. This was another part of its appeal in such a macho society as the Roman army. Secret societies with their hidden rites and private languages make their members feel special, a cut above others. And there's something about belonging to an exclusive club that seems to appeal to a certain kind of man. Mithraism had all of that in spades.

The emergence of these mystery cults in the Roman Empire was a turning point in religious history. Before it, religion had been mainly a group activity attached to a common identity. For Jews their religion was what they were by birth and God's summons to them as a special people. Their moral seriousness often attracted outside sympathisers, but gentiles or foreigners could not change the accident of their birth. Hinduism was also something you were born into, down to the caste you were stuck in. So far Buddhism had been the only exception to this rule. It had challenged the destiny of the group and offered its version of salvation to individuals. And by this time in Asia it was on the way to becoming a *universal* religion, a religion for anyone, anywhere, at any time.

The interesting thing is that religions that offer help to private individuals are likely to grow and become universal, because the world is full of individuals searching for salvation. The mystery cults showed this trend at work. Individuals *volunteered* to join them. This began to shift the idea of religion as a group identity and replaced it with the idea of personal conversion. And the methods the cults used to give their followers the emotional experience of salvation supplied a pattern that would be copied by religions yet to be born. The idea of a god who died and rose again appealed to something in human nature, especially if it offered people a way of rising from their own graves.

It would take a few centuries before these trends reached their highest expression in the history of religion. But the scene was being set for the appearance of the world's most populous and dominant religion. When Christianity was at its most successful it called itself *Catholic*. The word comes from Greek and means *universal*. And its founding belief was in the dying and rising of its god. In the next chapters we'll explore how what started as a tiny Jewish sect in the first century was transformed into the first truly universal religion – the Catholic Church – and how it earned itself that title.

CHAPTER 18

The Convert

The convert is another stock character in the drama of religion. *Conversion* means turning round and facing in the opposite direction. Most people change their opinions over the years, but it is normally a gradual process, a slow drift. Religious conversion is rarely like that. Converts can change in the blink of an eye. They do a U-turn on a dime. It's so sudden they say afterwards it was like being born again.

The birth analogy is apt because it reminds us that it takes time for a baby to come to term, no matter how quick the delivery. In the same way the *moment* of conversion may be sudden, but it is actually often the climax to a process that's been going on for years. Converts are divided souls, struggling against something they can't admit they're attracted to. If they give in, it will take their life in a direction they don't want. So they fight, sometimes literally, against the very thing they are longing to submit to.

Of the many converts to Christianity whose lives were turned round by what happened to them, the most famous was a Jew called Saul who went on to become a Christian called Paul. His conversion is so famous that where it happened has gone into the language as shorthand for a sudden change of mind. When we want to describe a moment in a life when it turned in the opposite direction we talk about a *Damascus road* experience because it was on the road to Damascus that Saul finally surrendered to Christianity, the faith he had spent years persecuting.

We don't know exactly when Saul was born, but it is reckoned to have been at the beginning of the Christian Era around year 2. His exact date of death is also uncertain, but a reliable tradition tells us he was martyred for his beliefs in Rome between 62 and 65. We know he was born in Tarsus, in the Roman province of Cilicia in what is now south-east Turkey. We are told that he was Jewish and that he had inherited Roman citizenship from his father. Paul was probably his Roman name. A tentmaker by profession, he was an educated man who spoke and wrote fluent Greek. His letters to the churches he founded are the earliest Christian documents we have. He seems to have received part of his education in Jerusalem under an important teacher called Gamaliel. And he tells us he was a Pharisee.

No matter how unified they claim to be, all religions are coalitions of different groups who hold their faith in different ways, sometimes *very* different ways. Judaism in Saul's time was no exception. The most common division in religion is between conservatives and progressives. Knowing their religion came from prophets who heard the voice of God and passed on its directions to humanity, conservatives limit the faith to the first phase of the original revelation. But progressives want to accept new developments and the claims of later revelations. In first-century Judaism these contradictory tendencies were represented by the *Sadducees*, the conservative party, and the *Pharisees*, the progressive party, the party Saul belonged to.

The biggest difference between them was belief in life after death, a subject that did not come up in early Judaism. Abraham's discovery was that there was only one God. Moses' discovery was the election by that God of the Jews as his special people and keepers of his law. That was the original essence of Judaism to which the Sadducees held strictly. They distrusted some of the ideas Jews were said to have picked up during their captivity in Babylon, such as belief in the resurrection of the dead and the handing out of rewards and punishments to the resurrected. Another import from Babylon they were thought to have rejected was belief in angels. Angels were claimed to be intermediaries between God and the human race. Described as 'bodiless intelligences' or minds without bodies, angels were used by God to deliver messages to his children on earth. To the Sadducees they were another unnecessary import. God didn't need messengers to get his word out. He was already everywhere and closer to everyone than their own breath.

That's not how the Pharisees saw things. They were progressives who refused to accept that God had stopped teaching his children about the mysteries of his being and his intentions for the world. Why should they believe God had used up all the knowledge he wished to impart to his people hundreds of years ago? Was he not a living God, able to call new prophets to teach new truths to his people? Hadn't the prophet Daniel told them that God had put the angel Michael in charge of Israel and that, after a time of trouble such as they had never known, they would be delivered and the dead would rise from their graves, some to everlasting life and some to everlasting shame? And didn't the suffering they were experiencing under Roman rule fit Daniel's description? Weren't they all hoping for the end Daniel promised and the coming of the Messiah who would bring it to pass?

It was a time of religious and political turmoil in Israel. Jerusalem was packed with groups looking for the one who would bring in the messianic age. But a triple danger faced any pretender who was acclaimed by the people as the one who was to come. Israel was run by an impatient set of Roman officials who were alert to the tiniest sign of revolt. As far as they were concerned Messiah was a fancy name for a rebel against Roman rule. And they knew how to handle rebels.

The priests who ran the Temple were also a danger to messianic pretenders. To the Romans they might be political rebels, but to the priests they were blasphemers who challenged their exclusive authority to define God's will. And they knew how to handle blasphemers.

The members of the royal family the Herods, whom the Romans had put in charge of the four territories into which they had divided Israel, were also a danger to messianic pretenders. To these minor royals clinging to the remnants of their power, messianic pretenders were a threat to their position. And they knew how to handle anyone who threatened their way of life.

One Passover a messianic pretender called Jesus had been executed by the Romans as a rebel, with the agreement of the high priest, who condemned him as a blasphemer, and the support of Herod Antipas, the ruler of Galilee, for whom he had become an unwelcome nuisance. But the trouble did not end with the crucifixion of the man they called Jesus Christ or Jesus the Messiah. And that's when Saul entered the story.

The followers of Jesus did not shut up about him after his death. They became bolder. They said they had proof he was the Messiah sent by God to prepare Israel for the coming of the end. After his death, he had appeared to them on different occasions in different places and told them to stay together and wait for his final return. This infuriated the priests who thought they'd got rid of this dangerous nuisance once and for all. So they recruited Saul the Pharisee to the Special Branch of the Temple Police and ordered him to hunt down and capture these so-called 'Christians' before they caused any more trouble. Saul was desperate for the job and set about it eagerly when he got it.

We have a description of him from this time. He was small, bald and bow-legged. He himself admitted that physically he was unimpressive. But there was something about him. It was there in his eyes. He had passion, intensity, a searcher's gaze. He burned with restless energy. And he could argue! This was the man who now wore the badge of the Christian-hunter. But remember, he was a Pharisee. Sadducees didn't believe anyone could rise from the dead so they dismissed the claims of the Christians as nonsense. Their logic was straightforward: no man can rise from the dead; Jesus was a man; therefore Jesus did not rise from the dead.

That's not how the Pharisees argued. They believed God would one day raise the dead for a final judgment. They just didn't believe he had already raised Jesus. And nor did Saul. That's why he was on the trail of the blasphemers who did believe it. But was there a bit of doubt in him? Is that why he was so vehement? In running all over the country chasing Christians was he running away from himself?

And run he did. He heard that there were already followers of Jesus in Damascus, over a hundred miles north of Jerusalem. Where would they get to next? He got authorisation from the high priest to hunt them down. As he travelled along the road to Damascus a great light blinded him and he fell to the ground. Then he heard a voice. 'Why are you persecuting me?' it asked. 'Who are you?' Paul cried back. 'I am Jesus whom you are persecuting', he was told. The voice then told him to get up and enter Damascus where he would be told what to do. When Saul got to his feet he was blind. Don't dismiss his blindness as a superstitious lie. Remember what the human mind can do. There's a saying: there's none so blind as those that will not see. Saul's blindness was the symptom of his long refusal to acknowledge what he now knew to be true. His assistants led him into Damascus and found a room for him. Blind and confused, he was there for three days, able neither to eat nor to drink, waiting to find out what would happen next.

A local disciple of Jesus called Ananias came to Saul in his lodgings in Straight Street and looked after him. His sight returned and he immediately did a dangerous thing. He went to the local synagogue and announced to the worshippers present that Jesus was the Son of God, the Messiah they were all looking for. He knew this, he informed them, because Jesus had appeared to him.

Imagine the effect of this on the disciples of Jesus. Their persecutor now claimed to be one of them. Was it a ruse? Had Saul gone undercover to infiltrate their movement the better to identify its members and convict them? They were nervous about their new convert.

Saul himself wasn't sure what to do next. What he decided was typical of him. Rather than turning to the leaders of the Church to find out about their beliefs and ask to be admitted, he went away by himself into Arabia to think and pray about what had happened to him. He needed nobody's instruction on the Christian faith, he thought. Jesus had given him all he needed by his appearance on the Damascus road. The resurrection of Jesus *was* the message. Get hold of that and you've got everything that matters.

It took another three years before Saul, now called Paul, made it to Jerusalem to meet the leaders of the Jesus movement. Or, as he would have put it, the *other* leaders of the movement. Because he too now claimed to be an apostle, meaning one *sent* by Jesus to proclaim his message. And they'd better get used to it.

Isn't it odd, thought the other apostles, that this upstart never met Jesus and knows nothing about his earthly life, yet here he is proclaiming his resurrection. *We* knew him, though he baffled us. We'd never heard anyone speak the way he did. Was he the Messiah, we wondered? We followed him to find out. But it didn't turn out the way we expected.

So who was this man called Jesus? And what really happened to him?

CHAPTER 19

The Messiah

The first thing to know about Jesus Christ is that Christ is not a surname. It's a title. *Christos* is the Greek translation of the Hebrew for Messiah. He was Jesus the Messiah. Except that not everyone agreed, so even his name was a source of controversy, a controversy that followed him to his death. When the Romans crucified him they kept the game going. Above his head on the cross they fixed a scoffing label: THE KING OF THE JEWS! He was just a joke to them, another crazy Jew trying to change the world.

From the beginning, people argued about him: where he came from, who his parents were, who he thought he was, and what happened to him after his death. They still do. Billions of words have been written about him. The earliest are in the Christian Bible or New Testament, so named to distinguish it from the Jewish Bible or Old Testament. That distinction is a clue to how his first disciples saw him. To them he did not come to start a new religion. He came to fulfil the old religion of the Jews. God had called Abraham and Moses to establish the first covenant or testament.

Now he had called Jesus to establish a new covenant and bring it to completion in the messianic age.

To find out about his life we have to go to the New Testament. Unfortunately, the way it is organised is misleading. It opens with four books called Gospels, a word that means good news. This is the order: the Good News according to Matthew, Mark, Luke and then John. Then a book called the Acts of the Apostles, followed by lots of letters, most of them by Paul the convert we met in the previous chapter. So why didn't I start the previous chapter with Matthew, the first piece of writing in the Christian Bible?

Because it isn't the first. The first or earliest we can be certain about is a letter Paul wrote to his Christian converts in the Greek city of Corinth in about 55, twenty-five years after the death of Jesus. It shows no interest in the *life* of Jesus, only in what happened to him after his death. Its message was that his death did not finish him. It delivered him to a new life in God from which he was able to be in touch with those left behind on earth. Paul lists hundreds of people to whom Jesus appeared after his death, including his own experience on the road to Damascus.

So the first thing the New Testament tells us about Jesus is that his death did not remove him from history. His appearances proved that his death was not the end of him. It was the beginning of God's promised new age, the opening shot in God's campaign to establish a new order in the world. And death wouldn't be the end for the disciples of Jesus either. If they died, they too would attain life after death. But they might not even have to die. The resurrection of Jesus proved that God was on the move at last. The perfect kingdom Jesus had described was about to be established on earth. And everything would be changed. Even death!

That letter from Paul to the Corinthians in 55 is the first snapshot we get of Jesus, and it covers only what happened after his death. To find out about his life we have to go to the Gospels, which came later. Mark came first, in the late 60s or early 70s. Matthew and Luke followed between 80 and 90. John brought up the rear around 100. These dates are worth noting. The further away in time you get from the life of a prophet the more the story gets embroidered and embellished. That's what happened to Jesus. I don't want to get into arguments about how or where he was born and how exactly he rose from the dead. Or about how many angels were present at his birth in Bethlehem or his resurrection in Jerusalem. I want to stick to the most generally accepted facts about him. They are compelling enough.

Mark plunges us straight into a scene of apocalyptic theatre. A wild man who lives on locusts and wild honey and wears a garment of camel hair comes out of the desert and starts preaching. They call him John the Baptiser because he plunges people into the river Jordan as a sign they are sorry for their sins and want a fresh start. They drown their old lives and rise to new ones. John does not claim to be the Messiah. But he says he has come to prepare the way for the one who is. Mark then tells us that a man from Nazareth in Galilee strode into the Jordan to be baptised by John. This is our first glimpse of Jesus in history. He is already thirty years old. It's what happened next that's the real start of his story.

When John pulled him back to the surface after holding him under water for a few long seconds, Jesus was dazzled by light and heard God calling him his beloved son. Though we can't be certain that that was the moment Jesus knew he was the Messiah, it was definitely when his mission began. Remember again what it is that prophets do. They hear the voice of God speaking to them and tell others what they have heard. And it puts them on a collision course with those who think they already know all there is to know about God. They are the religious experts. They are not going to take lessons from a country boy from Galilee. Three points of collision between Jesus and the official representatives of Judaism tell us all we need to know about the forces that drove him to his death.

The first is in Mark. He tells us that after his baptism Jesus started ministering to the poor and the suffering. The official view of suffering as punishment for sin outraged him and so did the fact of suffering itself. Suffering was not caused by the way God had ordered the world. It was caused by the way the powerful in religion and politics had organised it. God hated what they had made of his world, so he had sent Jesus to show what his kingdom would be like when it came on earth. It would be good news for the poor. And it would release God's children from the ropes the legalists had tied round their lives.

His first public collision with the authorities came over the commandment to keep the Sabbath as a day of rest. Jesus was leading some of his disciples through a field of wheat. They plucked the odd head of grain to chew as they walked and the Pharisees accused them of working on the Sabbath because they had picked the grain. Jesus's reply was revolutionary. The Sabbath, he said, was made for humanity not humanity for the Sabbath. We need rules and regulations in society, but they are our servants not our masters. If we impose them too strictly they become more important than the people they were designed to help. The fact that the Taoists had recognised this six hundred years before shows just how tenacious legalism is. Now Jesus was challenging it again. Law should be subject to humanity, not humanity to law. No wonder the legalists hated him. That was the first count against him. Down it went on the charge sheet.

The second collision, the Sermon on the Mount, came in Matthew and it was more dangerous. Jesus challenged the way the powerful ran the world. The theory was that humans were a chaotic rabble who needed to be kept under control. Give them an inch and they would take a mile. So strike them hard and strike them often. The fist on the jaw and the boot on the back of the neck is the only language they understand. Yet Matthew has Jesus standing on a mountain like Moses with the Ten Commandments describing what it will be like when God's kingdom comes on earth.

If someone slaps you on one cheek, you will turn the other so that he can slap that as well. If someone takes your jacket, you'll offer him your coat as well. You will love your enemies, not hate them. You will do good to those who do evil to you. And you will forgive and forgive and forgive and forgive . . . endlessly. That's how it is in heaven so that's how it should be on earth. The key to the downside-up kingdom Jesus describes here is in the word said to him at his baptism: 'you are my beloved son'. God was not ruler, not boss, not warden of the human jail, not slave driver but *father*! And the human race was one family. Revolutionary talk! Small wonder the rulers kept an eye on him. This was the second count against him. Down it went on the charge sheet.

The third collision is described in Luke. Jesus never gave lectures telling people what to think. Like the prophets of Israel he told stories that made people think for themselves. A friendly listener had asked him to repeat the most important commandments in the Jewish law. Jesus replied that they were to love God with all their heart, soul and might. That was the first commandment. The second was to love their neighbours as themselves. Correct, replied the listener, but who is my neighbour? The parable of the Good Samaritan was his answer.

A man fell among thieves who left him naked and unconscious on a dangerous and deserted road. A priest came along followed by his assistant. They were good men who wanted to help, but their religion prevented it. The man at the side of the road might be dead. According to their religion, touching a dead body would pollute them. And the injured man might belong to a race Jews were not allowed to associate with. So touching him might make them unclean. They pass by on the other side and leave him lying there. Next along is a Samaritan, one of the races Jews were forbidden to associate with. His religion has the same prohibitions as theirs, but his compassion at the man's plight overrides his religion. He goes to the man's aid and saves his life. According to Jesus, a neighbour is not someone on your religious team. A neighbour is anyone who needs your help. If God is our father and we are his children then *everyone* is my neighbour, my sister and my brother.

It's easy to miss the target of this parable. Law was the target of the saying about the Sabbath in Mark. Power politics was the target of the Sermon on the Mount in Matthew. And in the story of the Good Samaritan *religion* is the target. Jesus was saying that the institution that claims to represent God can easily become God's greatest enemy, because it rates its own rules higher than God's love. No wonder the priests hated him and started building a case against him. This was the third count against him. Down it went on the charge sheet and the case against him was complete. It was now only a matter of time before they came for him.

Jesus had taught his disciples a prayer. It was short but into its few lines was packed everything he had ever taught them. *Our father who art in heaven*, it began, *thy will be done, thy kingdom come on earth as it is in heaven*. It's been around so long it's lost its punch even for Christians who still use it. But imagine its impact if you were a priest who thought he already served God on earth; or if you were a political ruler trying to keep an unruly colony under control? It was fighting talk. Enough to get a man killed.

CHAPTER 20

Jesus Comes to Rome

They came for Jesus in the middle of the night. That's when the secret police always come. When the city is quiet and human energy is at its lowest, they strike. They arrested him in a private garden, led there by one of his own.

Jesus had been a master of the symbolic gesture. When he started his movement of spiritual liberation he echoed the entry of the Jewish people into Canaan. The Bible tells us that the Jews who fought their way out of Egypt into the Promised Land were divided into twelve clans, known as the Twelve Tribes of Israel. So Jesus chose twelve men from among his band of disciples to help him lead his very different campaign. He called them *apostles*, a Greek word that means messengers. Their message was the good news that God's kingdom of peace was at hand.

But the apostles were not an impressive bunch. The two most famous of them turned out to be failures, Peter and Judas. Peter was affectionate but weak. He deserted Jesus after he was arrested, but it was Judas who led the police to the place where Jesus was hiding. We're not sure why he did it. The priests paid him thirty pieces of silver for his betrayal, but it seems unlikely that he did it for the money. Maybe he was disappointed that Jesus was not the kind of Messiah he had expected. Jesus had an enormous following among the poor and oppressed in Israel, yet he hadn't taken up the sword against the Romans. Would a push provoke him to call them to arms to bring in the promised kingdom? Was that Judas's motive? We don't know. Maybe he didn't know either. Matthew tells us that what happened to Jesus after his arrest in the Garden of Gethsemane broke Judas's heart and he hanged himself. It was too late to undo his action. By then Jesus was in the hands of the Roman soldiers.

The Roman soldiers were also masters of the symbolic gesture. After the authorities had sentenced Jesus to death by crucifixion, the soldiers pressed a crown of thorns on his head and wrapped him in an old cloak of imperial purple. 'Hail, King of the Jews', they mocked, as they led him to the place of execution. Crucifixion, slow death by impalement on a cross, was Rome's fiercest punishment. Its victims could hang for days before they died. When Spartacus led a rebellion of slaves against Rome in 73 BCE it was put down with terrible ferocity. When it was over, the Roman General Crassus crucified six thousand of the rebels and left them hanging for months along one of the great roads into Rome. It was quicker for Jesus. He lasted only six hours on the cross, probably because they'd whipped him so severely after his arrest he was half dead by the time they nailed him to the wood.

What was he thinking as he hung there? Had he been deceived by what he thought God had told him? Or did he accept his death as part of God's plan? Both suggestions have been offered. According to one theory, Jesus was convinced that when he reached the moment of maximum danger in his challenge to the authorities God would act. It's not unlike the theory about Judas trying to force the hand of Jesus. Was Jesus trying to force God's hand? Did he think that by proclaiming a kingdom that was not like anything that had ever been seen on earth, and being prepared to die for it, God would erupt into history and turn the tables on the rulers of this world? If that's what he expected, it didn't happen.

There was no rescue from the Romans. No sudden swoop by God into history to end its suffering. There was only the cross and the certainty that he would die on it. What had he achieved? Nothing! Mark tells us that before his last breath Jesus cried out in despair, 'My God, my God, why hast thou forsaken me?'

The other Gospel writers gave the crucifixion of Jesus a different twist. Jesus, they suggested, was always in control. His death was part of God's plan from the beginning. He knew it was part of the deal. And by the time John's Gospel was written this had become the official story. In John the last word of Jesus is not a cry of despair as in Mark, but a shout of triumph: 'It is accomplished!'

It doesn't look as if any of his followers had expected what happened next. Apart from a small group of loyal women, they all deserted him when the police came for him. They feared they'd be next. And they waited for the knock on the door in the hopeless hours before dawn. But it never came. What came surprised them. It was Jesus who came, though they might not have been able to say exactly how they knew it. In his letter to the Corinthians Paul described the surprise of it all. And he gives a list of all the people to whom Jesus appeared. Last of all, he says, he appeared to me. And we are back to that incident on the road to Damascus. That was the next surprise to hit the apostles.

The appearances of Jesus had emboldened Peter and the other apostles. They had scattered at his arrest, but now they were back together again and Peter was showing more courage. Though they weren't sure how the future would unfold, they started telling their fellow Jews what had happened. With increasing boldness they repeated their belief that Jesus, though he had suffered a form of death the Bible said was cursed, was the promised Messiah. His appearances were the proof.

But what was the timetable for the new kingdom they now believed was on its way? It couldn't be delayed much longer, they thought. They would all live to see it. And there would be no mistaking it this time. When Jesus came back it wouldn't be secretly as in the appearances after his death. Next time it would be in the full majesty of his kingdom. Paul had found the best way to express it. He said the resurrection of Jesus after his death had been the first sheaf of a mighty harvest that would soon be gathered in.

The original disciples of Jesus still didn't know what to make of Paul. From being their greatest persecutor, Saul now called Paul had morphed into their most irritating nuisance. After they got over the shock of his conversion, after they permitted him to call himself an apostle because he'd been 'called' by Jesus on the road to Damascus, he was still a hard man to deal with. Like Jesus, the disciples were all Jewish and wanted things to stay that way. Whatever his return involved and whenever it happened, they were certain it would be in Jerusalem, God's holy city. That's why they wanted to sit tight where they were and wait for him. They would go on spreading the news that he was the Messiah and would be back soon, but only among Jews, only among his own people.

'No!', Paul thundered. Don't you realise that God has torn up that old deal and published a new one? The old had served its purpose and it had been a glorious purpose. But it was over. It was like having to go to school as a child. Very important when you're young but it ends when you grow up. And there was something else. The new deal wasn't just for Jews. It was for everyone. It was for the whole world!

You shouldn't just huddle together in Jerusalem waiting passively for the return of Jesus, Paul told them. You should be out there telling the world that you don't need to be Jewish to follow the way of Jesus. We, of course, will continue to be faithful Jews in our observances. That's our heritage. But surely you are not going to tell gentiles that if they want to follow Jesus they have to get themselves circumcised because circumcision has been the way Jewish boys have been marked as God's own for centuries? That was then. This is now. What's needed now is not circumcision of the foreskin but circumcision of the heart. *Spiritual* circumcision! Gentiles must cut themselves off from their old way of living and start to live in the spirit of Jesus. And we haven't got much time to get the message out. He'll be back sooner than you think. Already people are dying who haven't heard the message. We've got to hurry, there's no time to lose.

On and on Paul went at them till he wore down their defences. But they didn't give in to him completely. They patched together a compromise. The original followers of Jesus would stay in Jerusalem. That's where they'd wait for his return. And they would remain faithful to all their Jewish customs and traditions. They would keep the full package. But Paul could go to the gentiles and tell them about Jesus. Any converts he made wouldn't be required to follow the traditions of Judaism. And go he did. He wore himself out in his travels round the Roman provinces at the eastern end of the Mediterranean where he made many gentile converts to Jesus and established churches wherever he went.

That is why it has been said that it was not Jesus but Paul who was the real founder of Christianity. Without him the Jesus movement would have faded as yet another failed messianic sect within Judaism. It was Paul who took it into history. True, but he took Jesus with him. It was Jesus he preached: the Jesus he'd met on the road to Damascus; the Jesus who'd revealed the good news of God's love for the world; the Jesus who would be back soon so there was no time to waste.

Except that Jesus didn't come back. He still hasn't come back, though the expectation that he will return one day has never gone away. And it is part of the official creed of Christianity where it says to this day 'he shall come again in glory to judge both the living and the dead'.

Paul had won the grudging respect of the other apostles and had been encouraged to develop his mission to the gentiles and plant his churches. It was a different business with the official authorities of Judaism. They had lost their most effective persecutor of Christians. They had commissioned him to put their enemy out of business, but he had switched his allegiance and joined them. Now *he* was the enemy. So they came after him with the same intensity that had sent him charging down the Damascus road. He was constantly arrested and punished. Five times he received the official punishment of thirty-nine lashes. On three occasions he was beaten with rods. On one occasion he was stoned. Finally, he'd had enough of it and appealed to the Roman authorities. He was a Roman citizen, after all, and as such he demanded a proper trial for his alleged offence in preaching the good news of Jesus.

The Roman authorities finally acknowledged that as a citizen his request was legitimate, so they brought him to Rome for trial. They placed him under arrest when he got there. But that didn't stop him making converts to his faith in Jesus. Paul was the kind of man who couldn't stop making converts to his cause, even in prison. Now Christianity had made it to Rome. It had happened quietly and beneath the radar, as this small, bow-legged man with the intense gaze took up residence in the capital city of the Roman Empire.

Events that come on tiptoe often change the world. This was one of them. And it would alter the course of history.

CHAPTER 21

The Church Takes Charge

There were probably Christians in Rome before Paul got there. The roads and seaways of the empire encouraged traffic in ideas as well as the movement of troops, so it is likely that Christians had already established themselves in the capital of the Roman world. Not that much attention would have been paid to them. Paul described the first Christians as despised and unimportant, the kind of beaten people who followed Jesus in Israel. And there would have been slaves among them. Slaves were human property owned by their masters like horses or the stables they stood in. Slavery was a universal fact of life. Even the Bible took it for granted. It was the way things were, like the wetness of water or the dryness of sand. One of the converts Paul had made while he was under arrest in Rome was a runaway slave called Onesimus, who had robbed his master and fled to the city. Paul loved him but he did not try to rescue him from slavery. He sent him back like a lost wallet to his owner Philemon, begging him to treat him kindly now that he was a fellow Christian.

Why didn't Paul challenge slavery as being against the Christian message of universal love? Why didn't he persuade Philemon to free his slave rather than just asking him to be nice to him now that he had him back? Probably because he didn't expect the world as it was to last much longer. Jesus would return soon to bring in God's kingdom of justice and love, so why tinker with a system that was on the point of extinction? If you are about to demolish a house you don't waste time fixing the plumbing. This meant that the first Christians did not seem to be entirely at home in the world. And their hope that it would end soon made the Romans suspicious of them. It gave them the impression that Christians hated human-kind. But it was not until they noticed something else about them that the Roman authorities began to make Christians a target for their anger.

Incense is the resin of tree gum mixed with aromatic herbs, and when it is burnt it releases a sweet-smelling smoke. In ancient reli-gion, burning incense to a god was a popular devotion. They prob-ably once thought that when the smoke ascended from the brazier its sweetness delighted the god above and won his approval. The Romans required their subjects to drop a few grains of incense into a brazier below an image of the emperor, exactly as if they were worshipping him as a god. It became a test of loyalty like saluting a flag or standing for the national anthem. Whether they actually believed the emperor was a god is doubtful, but the practice certainly implied it. It was too much for the Christians. They protested that though they were loyal subjects of the emperor they could not burn incense to him as if he were a god.

That did it for the authorities. The rumour that Christians were scheming to bring the world to an end, alongside their stubborn refusal to burn incense to the emperor, provoked a series of persecutions that punctuated the next few centuries. The first started in 64 when Nero was emperor. A terrible fire had broken out in Rome and with it the rumour that the emperor had started it to clear the way for an extension to his palace. And it was said that he had stood on his balcony playing his fiddle while the city burned below him.

Alarmed by the danger that now threatened him, Nero foisted the blame onto the Christians. Everyone knew how they hated the emperor and wanted the world to end. They were the guilty ones. An ugly persecution broke out. It was reported that Nero coated some Christians in oil and set them ablaze like candles in the palace gardens. We can't be certain, but it is likely that Paul was beheaded during this first official persecution of the Church. And there's a tradition that the Apostle Peter was in Rome at the time and he too was executed. Legend tells us that Peter asked to be crucified upside-down because he had deserted his master Jesus when they arrested him.

The persecutions did nothing to slow the expansion of Christianity. The reverse was true, as it often is when authority tries to stamp out something it doesn't approve of. The persecuted Christians claimed that the blood of the martyrs was the seed of the Church. And over the next two and half centuries the Church grew throughout the empire. Before moving on, it is worth noting that the word *Church* has two meanings. It translates a Greek word meaning an assembly or body of people. So the Christian Church means the people who follow Christ. Inevitably, the buildings they met in became known as churches. The best way to distinguish the two meanings is to give a capital 'C' to the people or assembly – Church. And a small 'c' to the building they meet in – church.

When the first Christians weren't avoiding their persecutors they spent a lot of time arguing with each other over their own beliefs. We've already seen that the Church's first dispute had been whether gentiles who converted to Christianity had to observe the Jewish code. Paul won that argument and set the scene for the expansion of the Church outside Judaism. It was a foretaste of more complicated rows to come. The next big argument was over who Jesus was. They knew he had been a man. They knew he came from Nazareth. They knew he died in Jerusalem. And they knew God had called him his beloved son. But how could he be both a man and God's son at the same time? Paul decided the issue by saying God had *adopted* him as his son. So did that mean there had been a time when he *wasn't* God's son? They didn't like that way of putting it. They preferred it the other way round. He had *always* been the Son of God, but some time around 4 BCE he had come into the world undercover to rescue his children. He had lived a human life for thirty-three years before being taken back into the Godhead. So he was fully God and fully man. But how exactly did all that work? They argued about it for centuries and it created rival camps and divisions.

Of course they did more than argue among themselves about the divinity of Jesus. They looked after the poor. They organised themselves efficiently, copying the administrative system of the Roman Empire. They split themselves into geographical units called *dioceses* over which supervisors or bishops were appointed. Under the bishops were priests who looked after local congregations. They had a third tier of welfare workers called deacons who looked after the poor and needy. It was an efficient set-up and it ran smoothly. Soon bishops in big cities like Rome became important figures, even in the eyes of the imperial authorities. Persecutions continued from time to time, but they only made the Church stronger. And the final persecution turned out to be the last grip of night before a new and surprising dawn.

While the Christian Church had been building itself into a formidably unified organisation, the Roman Empire had been going in the opposite direction. It had been tearing itself apart. Its armies had spent more time fighting among themselves than guarding the empire against the invaders who were hammering at its gates. But from time to time, strong leaders emerged who tried to stop the empire's decline. One of the strongest was called Diocletian. He became emperor in 284. In his attempts to unify the empire he unleashed the final and most ferocious persecution of the Church, because he saw it not as an ally but as a rival to his cause. The terror started in 303 and was awful while it lasted, but it was no more successful than those that had come before. And within ten years the situation was reversed and Church and empire were at one.

When Diocletian fell ill in 305 he resigned as emperor. Soon rival claimants to the leadership of the empire were again at war with each other. The most calculating and capable of the rivals was called Constantine. In 312, on the eve of the battle outside Rome that would decide who became the emperor, Constantine was in his tent sleeping when he had a vivid dream. In the dream he saw the Christian symbol of the cross glowing in front of him and he heard a voice commanding him: 'In this sign conquer!'

Next morning he had banners made, emblazoned with the sign of the cross, and he marched into battle behind them and defeated his rival. The following year he rescinded the decree persecuting Christians and allowed unlimited freedom of religion throughout the empire. In 315, he abolished crucifixion, which had been so loathed by Christians. And by 324, while other religions were still tolerated, he had established Christianity as the official religion of the empire. From persecuted outcast to the emperor's favourite religion in twenty years was an astonishing reversal.

But it would be naïve to see Constantine's move as a spiritual conversion to faith in Jesus. He was a calculating politician who had decided that Christianity could be the glue that held his empire together: a universal Church imprinted on a universal empire. But he was annoyed that the Church itself was divided into rival factions arguing about the best way to define the nature of Jesus Christ as God and man. The resolution of the dispute had come down to a detail so minute it actually hung on a single letter: *iota* the Greek letter for *i*. Determined to resolve the quarrel, in 325 Constantine summoned the bishops and their theologians to a great council in a town called Nicaea in what is now Turkey. He locked them in a room and refused to release them until they'd resolved the issue. Was the *iota* to be in or out? In the event they decided against the *iota* and took it out of the word at the centre of the dispute. The issue was resolved and the double nature of Jesus Christ as both fully God and fully man was finally defined.

Constantine was so delighted with the outcome that he invited the bishops to join him at an imperial banquet. He ordered his bodyguard to line up with drawn swords outside the entrance to his palace and the bishops solemnly processed into the imperial apartments where they dined in style on couches suitably arranged around the banqueting hall. One bishop was so thrilled with the occasion that he described it as a picture of Christ's Kingdom come at last on earth. But it was not a picture Jesus would have recognised. The very power that had crucified him had now decided to recruit him for its own purposes.

Historians have seen this event as the final triumph of the Church over its persecutors and the beginning of its long domination of European history. It now called itself the Catholic (or universal) Church because it was spread throughout the Roman world. As the power of the empire declined, the power of the Church increased, until it reached a stage when it was the most powerful institution on earth and kings cringed before its authority. Its partnership with the world of political power became known as Christendom or Christ's Realm. And so powerful was Christendom at its height that it was almost impossible to see through the clouds of glory that covered it to the bleeding form of the peasant from Galilee who had started it all. Almost, but not quite impossible. Because though it was now a real crown he had upon his head and a real cloak of imperial purple in which he was wrapped, when they came to church for worship Christians continued to hear descriptions of the other Christ from the New Testament. He never did come back as he had promised he would. But there were always those in the Church who thought that was because he had never really gone away.

The Christian story was far from over. Its greatest years were yet to come. But we'll leave it for a few chapters to look at the rise of another religion that looked back to Abraham as its father: Islam.

CHAPTER 22

The Last Prophet

Three religions claim Abraham as their fore-father. And there are two ways to understand the claim. It can be taken as a form of spiritual descent. Abraham passed his monotheism to the Jews and through them to the Christians. Then in the seventh century Islam reclaimed it from what it perceived to be its dilution by both these religions. But the descent from Abraham can also be understood in a physical sense. Abraham's son Isaac was the father of Israel, through whom Jews and Christians trace their paternity. But Abraham had another son. And thereby hangs a tale.

Abraham had two wives, Sarah and her Egyptian handmaid Hagar. Sarah was jealous of Hagar. She was afraid Abraham would appoint Hagar's son Ishmael as his heir. So she persuaded her husband to banish them both. Hagar took her young son and wandered with him into the desert not far from the Red Sea, where she sat down on a rock and wept, because she was so sad and unhappy. But Ishmael was not sad and unhappy. He was angry, very angry. In his fury, according to Islamic tradition, he started kicking the sand. He kicked it so hard he uncovered a spring of water of the sort that is found in green spots in the desert called oases. When Abraham heard about the oasis Ishmael had created, he visited the wife and son he had discarded and built a temple near the spring that had saved their lives. In the temple he installed a sacred black stone. On which hangs another tale.

Genesis, the book that opens the Jewish Bible, tells us that the first man was called Adam and his wife was called Eve. Adam and Eve lived in a wonderful garden called Eden where they lacked for nothing. Of all the fruit trees in the garden, only one was forbidden to them. This was the Tree of the Knowledge of Good and Evil. Adam and Eve lived a life of unchanging childlikeness, their every need met by God. Parents sometimes think they'd like to keep their children young for ever. But the children can't wait to grow up and discover the knowledge of good and evil for themselves. That was the urge that prompted Adam and Eve to eat of the forbidden fruit. And their minds were immediately flooded with the knowledge that life was no longer simple.

Now that Adam and Eve had lost their innocence, God sent them out into the world to live life in all its adult complexity. But, in Islam's account of the story, he allowed them to take something from the garden as a memento. It was to serve as a reminder both of what they had left behind forever and of what would be with them forever. They had lost Eden but they had not lost God. God would still be with them when the gates of Eden closed behind them. What they took with them was a black stone said to have come down from heaven. Abraham had inherited the stone and this is what he now installed in the Kaaba or temple at the oasis Ishmael had discovered. A city grew round the Kaaba with its fabled Black Stone. The city's name was Mecca.

Mecca (in what is now Saudi Arabia) was halfway down the eastern shore of the Red Sea in Arabia, one of the most mysterious and fascinating parts of the earth. Arabia is a huge peninsula, 1,200 miles long and 1,300 miles broad, bounded on the west by the Red Sea, on the south by the Arabian Sea and on the east by the Persian Gulf. In the vast deserts of the interior lived clans of nomads or Bedouin who were resolute and fiercely independent warriors.

Genesis nailed it when it described Ishmael as 'a wild ass, his hand against every man and every man's hand against his'. Though the rival clans of the Bedouin fought and squabbled with each other over the ownership of wells and oases, they all revered the Holy City of Mecca and made pilgrimages to kiss the Black Stone handed down by Adam and to drink of the well discovered by Ishmael. Their grandfather Abraham had been a passionate mono- theist but the same could not be said of them. Though they worshipped Allah as their High God, they also loved their idols and had one for every day of the year. And so did the merchants who made a good living out of the pilgrims who came to kiss the Black Stone and drink from the waters of the Sacred Well and buy idols from the shops that had multiplied round the Kaaba.

Abraham – as the old Hebrew account told us – had known how easy it was to make a business out of religion. He'd watched his father make idols to sell in the family shop, idols he had denounced as a scam to fleece the poor of their pennies. He would have hated what was going on in Mecca where its merchants were exploiting the needs of the pilgrims who came seeking spiritual comfort. This always happens in holy cities, no matter the century or the denom- ination. A fast buck can always be made selling spiritual consola- tion to the needy. Jesus had hated what he saw in Jerusalem where the priestly families made fortunes out of the poor. That's why he overturned the tables of the money-changers in the Temple and told them they had turned the House of God into a den of robbers. A man was born in Mecca in 570 who became as angry as Jesus at the corruption of the monotheism of Abraham by the hucksters and peddlers of his native city. His name was Muhammad.

Muhammad hadn't had an easy life. His father had died before he was born and his mother when he was six. The young orphan was looked after by his grandfather until he was adopted by his uncle Abu Talib, a successful businessman, who put the young Muhammad to work as a camel driver. Caravan trains of camels laden with goods were a feature of the economy of Arabia. They would plod their way north to Syria, west to Egypt and Palestine and east to Persia, carrying perfumes and spices, which they'd exchange for silk and linen before making the long journey home. The prophet Isaiah had described multitudes of camels from Sheba in southern Arabia bringing gold and frankincense to Jerusalem. This was the kind of work Muhammad was apprenticed to.

He was a quick learner and his reputation for competence and trustworthiness prompted a wealthy widow called Khadija to put him in charge of one of her caravans to Syria. Muhammad and Khadija married in 595 when he was twenty-five and she was forty. They had six children: four daughters, and two sons who died in infancy. Fatima would be his most famous daughter. She would marry Ali and become the mother of Hasan and Husayn, Muhammad's grandsons. Muhammad was a successful trader, but his reputation for honesty and fair dealing also meant that he became the kind of community leader people turned to when they needed help solving business disputes and family squabbles. But that wasn't all there was to Muhammad.

He belonged to that special group who constantly look through or beyond this world to find its meaning and purpose. They are troubled by the ugliness and injustice that characterises human society. And while they respect the way religion puts struggling humans in touch with spiritual realities beyond themselves, they also know how easy it is for the powerful to manipulate religion for their own ends and against the good of the people it is meant to help.

Disgusted with the rackets he witnessed in the Kaaba at Mecca, when he was about forty years old Muhammad started going away by himself to pray and meditate in a cave outside Mecca. It was there he saw his first vision and heard his first voice, visions and voices that continued for the rest of his life. He was aware they did not come directly from God. They came through the mediation of the angel Gabriel. Gabriel's first words to him had been: 'Recite in the name of your Lord who created; created man from an embryo'. Muhammad didn't know what to make of it. Had he heard the voice of an evil spirit tempting him? Or was he going mad? Isn't that what is always said of those who see visions and hear voices? So Muhammad was filled with confusion and uncertainty. But the voice continued to speak to him in words of great beauty and fascination. And he became convinced it was calling him to be a prophet.

The whole point of prophets is that they don't keep what they hear to themselves. They are sent to warn the world and persuade it to listen to what God has told them. So after a few years listening to the angel Gabriel's revelations – revelations he had memorised and could recite by heart – and with the warm support and encouragement of his wife Khadija, in the year 613 Muhammad began to preach to the men and women of Mecca. There was nothing original about his message and Muhammad never claimed there was. It was a reminder of what they had forgotten. It was the message of the prophet Abraham: idols were dupes and there was no God but God.

Muhammad's message was particularly attractive to the poor because they were the ones being ripped off by the merchants who ran the shrine and sold the idols. Soon he had a following in Mecca of those 'who had surrendered themselves to God', which is the meaning of the word Muslim. Things were fine as long as he stuck to his message that there was no God but Allah and Muhammad was his prophet. Religions are a dime a dozen and there's always room for another in the spiritual market place. The game changes when the new creed starts threatening the profits and privileges of the established set-up. That's what happened here. Muhammad denounced the traders who made fortunes out of the idol market beside the Kaaba and those who charged pilgrims to drink from the sacred well. The inevitable followed. A persecution of Muslims broke out in Mecca.

Fortunately, a deputation of visitors from the city of Yathrib who had heard Muhammad preach invited him to move there with his followers. The men from Yathrib knew their city needed a leader and here was just the man, they thought. The move to Yathrib, just over two hundred miles from Mecca, was accomplished in secret. Muhammad, his cousin Ali and friend Abu Bakr were the last to leave. They left Mecca by night and their escape in September 622 became known as the *Hegira* or flight. It is the moment that begins the first year of the Muslim calendar. The city of Yathrib to which they escaped was later given the new name Medina, or City of the Prophet.

The move did not settle matters, and for the next ten years there were battles between Mecca and Medina. Finally, in 630 Muhammad marched with a large army against his native city. Realising the game was up, the Meccans surrendered and the Prophet entered the city. There were no reprisals against the inhabitants, but Muhammad removed the idols from the Kaaba and encouraged the citizens of Mecca to become Muslims. He then returned to Medina.

But his death was close. In 632 he made a pilgrimage to Mecca and preached his Farewell Sermon. This farewell visit of Muhammad's to the Kaaba in Mecca with its Black Stone and Sacred Well celebrated and confirmed the *Hajj* or pilgrimage as one of the five duties – the Five Pillars of Islam – that Muslims are meant to fulfil. The Prophet did not long survive the Hajj. He fell ill with a fever and died on 8 June 632. But he left behind him a faith that is now the second largest religion in the world and continues to make its mark on history. In the following chapters we'll explore something of the richness of its theology and practice.

CHAPTER 23

Submission

Before taking a look at the beliefs and practices of *Islam* – an Arabic word that is the root of the word Muslim and is best translated as 'submission to the will of God' – we ought to capture a difference between it and its close relatives, Judaism and Christianity. The first principle of monotheistic religion is the reality of God. We could push it further by saying that for monotheism the *only* reality is God.

Think about the universe: millions of galaxies and maybe millions of universes we cannot see. There was a time when they weren't there. What *was* there, according to monotheism, was God. Everything that came into being came from God, the way characters in a novel come into existence through the mind of the author. I used the idea of humans as characters in a novel when discussing Hinduism. I want to use it again here when thinking about monotheism, but with a different spin. In Hinduism the spin was that the characters in the novel discovered that they had no real existence. They were an illusion. In the Abrahamic religions the characters exist all right, but they want to find out more about the one who created them, the author of their being.

Remember, you don't have to believe or accept any of this, but if you want to understand religion you have to get your mind into its way of thinking, if only for as long as it takes you to read this chapter. Monotheistic religion is like the characters in a book trying to make contact with their author. Even thinking about it makes you dizzy, doesn't it? Some characters in the book of the universe say it's obvious someone created us and it's natural for us to want to get in touch with whoever did it. Others say: don't be silly. There's no author, only the book itself, the universe or what-ever name you give it. It just happened. It wrote itself. So stop trying to get in touch with your imagined author.

But for those who insist on getting in touch the process is like any other creative activity. The prophets or sages wait and listen and look into the distance. They open themselves so that the source of their being will reveal itself to them. And its reality forms in their minds the way a character realises itself in the mind of an author. Except that this is the other way round. This is a character realising its author. Slowly a picture of God emerges like a photo-graph being developed in a dark room. Theologians call this activity emerging revelation. And they usually claim that the picture of God promoted by their faith is more advanced in its development than any previous version. Judaism is a better like-ness than polytheism. Christianity is better defined than Judaism. But Islam claims to possess the perfect portrait, superseding all that came before it. So let us continue our exploration of Islam with what makes it differ most from Judaism and Christianity: the Qur'an.

Don't think of the Qur'an as Islam's Bible. There are three big differences. The first is that the Bible was slowly put together over centuries by many different writers and editors. The second is that the Bible is a library, not a single book. And third, though it *contains* revelations from God, the Bible is known to be a *human* creation, formed by human hands. Islam does not accept any of these as descriptions of the Qur'an. It came to *one* man during his lifetime as a continuous stream of revelation. And while it was mediated *through* a man it is not a human creation. Like a cable that brings electricity into a building, Muhammad was the conduit of the Qur'an but its power came from God. The Qur'an is God's mind in earthly form, God's presence on earth. In fact the Qur'an is to Muslims what Jesus Christ is to Christians. Christians came to believe that Jesus was the incarnation of God on earth, God made available to the world in human form. Well, that's what the Qur'an is to Muslims. It is God with them. The word Qur'an means recitation. It was recited by the angel Gabriel into the ear of the Prophet. It was recited by the Prophet to his followers before it achieved its written form after his death. And devout Muslims still memorise it so that they can recite its 114 chapters or *suras* from beginning to end today.

Muhammad believed that what had started with the Jews and evolved further with the Christians had been fulfilled in his ministry. The Qur'an described him as 'the Seal of the Prophets'. There were to be no more prophets. The prophetic sequence was over. It was sealed. And Islam was its perfect summation. Muhammad was disappointed that Jews and Christians did not see things that way, although there was nothing unusual in their reaction. The keepers of an old religion are always reluctant to admit that their day is over and they should make way for the new. Muhammad had hoped to persuade the Jews and Christians of Medina not that he was their nemesis but that he was their fulfilment, the end they had been waiting for. As it says in the Qur'an, 'He has sent down upon thee the Book with the truth, confirming what was before it, and He sent down the Torah and the Gospel aforetime'. That's why Muhammad had first instructed his followers to turn in the direction of Jerusalem when they prayed. It was only after the Jews and Christians had rejected him as their prophet that he instructed his followers to turn towards Mecca instead.

But he believed their rejection of him, tragic though it was, was consistent. The Jews had always rejected the prophets God had sent to them. Their last rejection was of the prophet Jesus. And even the Christians had rejected Jesus by turning him into a god.

A passionate believer in the unity of God, Muhammad was outraged that not only had the Christians given God a son, they had manufactured two other deities to sit alongside God in heaven. This was because Christians had evolved a theory of God as a Trinity, or One God expressed in three different ways: as the Father in Creation at the beginning of the world; as the Son in Jesus Christ during his life on earth; and as the Spirit to guide humanity through history until the end of time. The Prophet thundered against this elaborate piece of theological engineering: *La ilaha illa Allah wa-Muhammad rasul Allah.*

Followers of Islam have to fulfil five principal duties as part of their faith, sometimes called the Five Pillars of Islam. The first duty is the sincere recitation of the *Shahada* or profession of faith in Arabic that ended the previous paragraph: 'There is no god but God and Muhammad is the prophet of Allah'. Recitation of this expression of monotheism is the form used by Muslims to assert their faith and by converts to Islam to confess it.

The second pillar is the requirement to pray five times a day to the One God, turned in the direction of Mecca. Called *salat*, the prayer is offered at daybreak, at midday, in the middle of the afternoon, at sunset and between sunset and midnight. One of the most haunting sounds on earth is the *muezzin* or crier calling believers to prayer from the high balcony on the minaret of a mosque. He faces each of the four directions of the compass in turn and cries: 'Allah is most great. I testify that there is no God but Allah. I testify that Muhammad is the prophet of Allah. Come to prayer. Come to salvation. Allah is most great'. Nowadays the call to prayer is likely to be a recording crackling unevenly over the bustle of a modern city. But to hear at daybreak the cry of the muezzin pouring itself over a silent African village is to be pierced with longing.

The third pillar is called *zakat* or the giving of alms. Since all wealth comes from the generosity of God, for devout Muslims to give alms is to give back to God what is already God's. It is also a way of helping the poor and needy as well as contributing to the mission of Islam. Islam is a missionary religion whose aim is the conversion of the world to its vision of a single community or *umma* in which faith and life are integrated into a seamless whole. In the umma there will be no point where religion ends and society begins or where society ends and religion begins. It will be one thing.

The fourth pillar is the month-long fast of *Ramadan*, the ninth month of the Islamic calendar. The fast is observed from sunrise to sunset for thirty days. No food or drink is taken. But it is not just a matter of giving up eating and drinking. Towards the end of Ramadan special programmes are developed at the mosque aimed at increasing the knowledge and spirituality of the faithful. And on the twenty-seventh day of Ramadan a special celebration called the Night of Power marks the first night in which Muhammad received the revelation from God in that cave outside Mecca. Ramadan climaxes in the *Eid ul-Fitr*, the feast that ends the fast. Eid is a time of rejoicing when family members visit each other and exchange presents.

The fifth duty is one we have already noted, the pilgrimage or Hajj to Mecca. Getting to Mecca is a bigger deal than praying five times a day or fasting during the month of Ramadan, so Muslims are only expected to make the pilgrimage once in their lifetime. Pilgrims visit Abraham's Kaaba, now a large cube-shaped building inside the Grand Mosque in Mecca. Moving in an anti-clockwise direction, pilgrims move round the Kaaba seven times. Then they go to two small hills called Safa and Marweh. Pilgrims either run or walk quickly between them to represent Hagar's distress as she sought water for her son in the hot desert, water Ishmael uncovered with his furious kicking. Another dramatic element of the Hajj is when pilgrims throw stones at three pillars that represent all the evil in the world. The experience of the Hajj is so intense and defining for Muslims that they are allowed to add its accomplishment as a title to their names, Hajji for men and Hajjah for women.

The precision of the five duties makes Islam a lucid and uncomplicated religion to follow. But its practice has two powerfully emotive characteristics. The first is a reverence for the Prophet Muhammad that approaches, but never quite reaches, actual worship. There is no god but God, after all, but *Muhammad is the prophet of Allah.* Muhammad is not to be worshipped – he is not a god – but he is so revered that when his name is used it is customary to follow it with the phrase 'peace be upon him'. This is why Muslims are shocked and angered when their prophet is mocked or vilified by unbelievers.

But Muslim devotion to Allah is on an altogether more exalted level than its reverence for the prophet of Allah. Islamic monotheism is fierce and passionate, but as well as constantly emphasising the Oneness of Allah, the Qur'an becomes lyrical when celebrating Allah's beauty. One of the most touching traditions in Islam is the gathering of descriptive epithets of Allah scattered throughout the Qu'ran into a list of what are called the Ninety-Nine Most Beautiful Names of Allah. Here are a few of them:

> Allah, the Name that is above every name . . .
> The Merciful, the most merciful of those who show mercy . . .
> The Compassionate, who is gentle and full of compassion . . .
> The Watcher, who keeps watch over his creation . . .
> The Pardoner, ever ready to pardon and forgive . . .

There is beauty and comfort in the Qur'an. But that is not all we find there. Even in Sura 13 there are warnings that in the world's relationship with Allah there are dangers as well as consolations. Here are two more of the Beautiful Names:

> The Afflicter, who sends affliction as well as blessings . . .
> The Avenger, who wreaks vengeance on sinners . . .

The Qur'an sings the beauty of Allah. It also thunders his anger at sinners and unbelievers. So it's time we looked at that side of Allah and its consequences for many.

CHAPTER 24

Struggle

As well as being a prophet Muhammad was a warrior who led his followers in battles against the opponents of Islam. He saw no contradiction in the roles. His wars were not fought for the thrill of battle or the delights of plunder, though no doubt many of his followers enjoyed both. War was an instrument of his spiritual purpose and if we are going to understand him – or any of the other religious leaders in history who used violence to achieve their ends – we must try to get inside his mind.

The first thing to get hold of is that for visionaries like the Prophet life on earth was not an end in itself, something to be enjoyed for its own sake. It was as fleeting and poignant as the cry of the muezzin. It was an opening flourish, a prelude to the main act waiting for us beyond death where the real show began. The purpose of our stay on earth was to determine how we would spend the life without end that was waiting for us on the other side.

Imagine you were given a cast-iron guarantee that if you endured a painful ordeal for a few minutes you would receive a billion dollars that had already been paid into your bank account and only needed your assent to activate. How would you respond? Would you endure the pain of seconds to win the riches that awaited you when it was over? The chances are that you might go for the deal.

That's the reasoning behind the violence that often marks religion. It is the ruthlessness of the surgeon who cuts us open not to hurt us but to save our lives. Some believers give their lives as martyrs for the sake of the bliss that awaits them on the other side. For others, it is their duty to inflict pain and death on the bodies of friends and strangers in order to protect the faith against their assaults. Like it or not, that's the logic behind the holy wars and cruel purges that are a constant feature of religious history.

Few were as expert at holy warfare as the Muslims who fought first to establish Islam among their immediate neighbours and then to the ends of the earth. A hundred years after Muhammad's death Islam had control of Syria in the north and Egypt in the west. From Egypt it spread along North Africa. In time it took control of Palestine and large chunks of Persia. Islam reached India and China. And it conquered Spain where it tolerated, though limited, the activity of Christians and Jews. There was a moment when it looked as if it might overwhelm the whole of Catholic Europe before being turned back. But I am less interested in the recitation of the battles it fought and the territories it won than in the theological justifications it offered for doing so. And one of them resonates loudly in the world today. It is the idea of *jihad* or struggle.

Jihad is seen by some Muslims as the unofficial Sixth Pillar of Islam. Indeed, the determined effort to observe the five duties is itself seen as jihad. The word means struggle or effort, whether it is the struggle to keep the faith and build a just society or the struggle to defend Islam against its enemies. Down the centuries jihad has been practised in both senses, and in its violent aspect it has even been used by Muslim against Muslim. Violent disagreement between adherents of the same religion is common in history. It only took the death of Muhammad for it to break out within the young Islamic community itself. The form it took tells us a lot about how religions organise themselves and the sort of things they fall out over.

The issue in question was who should succeed the Prophet and on what principle should the appointment be made. What happened was that Muhammad's friend and loyal colleague Abu Bakr was elected as the first *caliph* or successor of the Prophet. Trouble started with the appointment of the fourth caliph who was Muhammad's own cousin and son-in-law Ali, husband of his daughter Fatima. Not everyone was in favour of Ali's appointment. It caused a split in Islam that continues to this day. There was a faction that wanted Muawiya, a cousin of the third caliph, to become fourth caliph rather than Ali, the Prophet's relative. In the struggle that followed Ali was killed and Muawiya took over. The champions of Ali then pressed for his son Husayn to be appointed, but in 680 Husayn too was killed in battle.

The conflict resulted in a division in Islam the technical term for which is a *schism*, a handy word for any students of religious history to incorporate into their technical vocabulary. Like many other useful terms, schism comes from the Greek and means to cut or snip. A schism is a group that cuts itself off from the main body and establishes its own sect or faction. Behind divorces like this there is usually a religious disagreement. One of the most common disagreements is over how spiritual leaders are appointed. In Christianity feuds over who were the genuine successors of the twelve apostles led to schisms in the Church that continue to this day, just like the splits in Islam.

The fracture in Islam resulted in two groups that became known as Sunnis and Shias. Sunnis were the larger group, Shias the schismatics who cut themselves off and established their own denomination. Sunni meant people who held to the original Sunna, or way of the Prophet. Shia meant the party of Ali, who believed the Prophet's successor had to be an *imam* or descendant of Muhammad. The fact that there are now numerous schisms within each of these original divisions reminds us just how brittle most religions are, especially when it comes to disputes about who's in charge.

Struggles over leadership in religious communities can be dismissed as examples of the human weakness for wanting to lord it over others. They highlight the earthly side of religion. They are sad but inevitable. Revealed religion, on the other hand, is supposed to take us right into the mind of God and the life of heaven. So it is disturbing to discover that the same compulsion to separate and divide will be present there as well. And life after death looks a lot like life before death. Remember, the Qur'an claims to show us what it is like on the other side when our earthly race is run. Two of the prospects offered should cause some of us to gulp with apprehension.

It tells us that everyone's final destination on the other side has already been fixed. The tickets have already been issued. In fact they were issued before we were born. This is called the doctrine of *predestination*. It's an idea found in other religious traditions, including Christianity. Wherever it is found it is disputed because of its apparent unfairness and cruelty. But let us take it first on its own terms. Most religions see life on earth as a preparation for what comes after death. The theory is that if we live good lives and follow the precepts of our faith – such as the Five Pillars of Islam – we will be rewarded by God and welcomed into Paradise. But according to one way of reading the doctrine of predestination God has marked everyone's paper before they've sat the exam. So why did God bother to send prophets to warn us to change our ways and work harder? Why struggle, why make the sacrifices of jihad, if our destiny is already fixed? We're back with our old friend the infallible author whimsically writing the fate of his characters, some to joy and success and others to misery and failure.

Here's how the voice that spoke to Muhammad expressed it in the Qur'an: 'We have put on their neck fetters up to their chin . . . we have put up before them a barrier and behind them a barrier . . . Alike it is to them whether thou hast warned them or whether thou hast not warned them, they do not believe.' To make it quite clear that the whole deal has been fixed in advance, there are other sacred writings in Islam that confirm it.

As well as the Qur'an, Muslims have a body of material called the *Sunnah* or way. If the Qur'an was what Muhammad heard from the angel Gabriel, the Sunnah is what Muhammad's close friends and family heard directly from him. It consists of *hadiths* or reports of his teaching and conversation. And it is in one of the Hadiths that we get the most explicit description of predestination: 'There is no one of you, no soul that has been born, but has his place in Paradise or in Hell already decreed for him, or, to put it otherwise, his unhappy or his happy fate has been decreed for him.' Gulp! How does that sit with some of those beautiful names for Allah as the Most Merciful, the Most Compassionate, the Pardoner who is always ready to forgive?

It doesn't sit at all well, which is why this teaching has been disputed by Islamic scholars almost since it was written down in the seventh century. If Allah is just, the scholars declared, then this doctrine of predestination contradicts his nature. The logic of religious struggle, such as the observance of the Five Pillars of Islam, implies that humans possess free will. Why would Allah send prophets to them if they were not free to listen, repent and follow in the way of salvation? So the arguments rolled.

The dispute reminds us that the interpretation of the Qur'an is less straightforward than may at first sight appear. It points to another source of vexation for students of religion. In all religions there is a group known as *literalists* who take sacred scriptures such as the Qur'an at their face value; whereas religious scholars, who usually know more about the texts than the literalists, are more subtle in their readings. They will often read as metaphor what literalists swallow as fact. The history of religious scriptures is the story of the long quarrel between these rival schools. Often it won't matter because the issue in dispute doesn't touch our lives. Sometimes it matters a lot because it can be the source of enormous fear and anxiety in the lives of ordinary people. If the idea of predestination is worrying enough, it is nothing compared to the allied doctrine of the existence of Heaven and Hell.

There are many suras in the Qur'an in which Heaven and Hell are mentioned. I'll give the most famous. In Sura 56, 'On the Day of Judgment', Paradise is described as a Garden of Delight that seems to have been designed for the exclusive enjoyment of the male of the human species. There are springs of wine permanently on tap that neither intoxicate nor cause a hangover. There are beautiful, wide-eyed young women available for the enjoyment of the new arrivals as a reward for the sufferings they endured on earth. More attractively, in Paradise there is no idle talk, only the saying 'Peace, Peace!' That's what waits for those the Qur'an calls 'Companions of the Right'. It's a very different deal for those it calls 'Companions of the Left'. It's Hell for them 'mid burning winds and boiling waters and the shadow of a smoking blaze . . .'

Heaven and Hell can be interpreted as metaphors, as a way of talking about the rewards of virtue or the consequences of vice. They can also be taken as literal fact. If Hell exists, it means that God consigns some of his children to an eternity of unendurable pain. We've already seen Hell making an appearance in other religions, so we'll close the Qur'an here. In the next chapter we'll think about humanity's grimmest invention and pay a visit to the region of boiling waters and smoking blaze. We'll look in on Hell.

CHAPTER 25

Hell

What is Hell? Hell is the place of everlasting torment to which sinners who have not repented are sent at death. In the full understanding of Hell that emerged in Christianity and Islam it is a place from which there is no escape. If you end up there, you are there for ever. That's the point.

So where is it? It is found in the human mind. Or in that part of it that creates the different worlds of religion. And to understand it we must remember how the religious imagination works. It operates on two levels. There is the thinking or wondering department. Humans can't help thinking about life and wondering what it means. Early on in their history they wondered about what happened to the dead. And they guessed the existence of an afterlife. They also wondered about the terrible inequality between people and decided that since it rarely got sorted in this life, if there was justice in the universe it would have to get sorted in the afterlife. Of course, they had no real information to go on about the afterlife when they decided all this. It was a guess or maybe just wishful thinking. But it came naturally from the musings of the human mind. That's why theologians called it *natural religion*.

Then the receiving department took over. This is the bit of the human mind that saw visions and heard voices. And it claimed to have received direct information about the afterlife. That's why this department of theology is described as *revealed religion*. Natural religion *wondered* what lay beyond the veil of death but revealed religion claimed to have *seen* it. But it's intriguing to note that though the questions were the same everywhere, the answers varied from region to region. The biggest difference was between Indian religion and Christianity and Islam.

To the sages of India the soul did not enter a permanent state after death. It was reborn into another life whose status depended on the merit it had increased or diminished in the life it had just left. There were hells and heavens in the Hindu tradition, but they were transit camps rather than final destinations. It might take millions of lives to escape the system, but there was always the hope that everyone would get out in the end. The ultimate goal was disappearance into nirvāna.

For those who lived further west their prospects were based not on the hope of final disappearance from the wheel of existence but on different versions of continuing life after death. An early appearance of the word *Hell* supplies a clue about what that might mean. In Anglo Saxon, the old language of England, Hell is the word for the Underworld, the abode of departed spirits. In the Old Testament it was called *Sheol*. But it wasn't a scary place. It was depressing. As we might say nowadays, 'it was depressing as hell'. Like people who never fully recover from a terrible illness, the dead in the Underworld hung around like wraiths waiting for something that never came.

But things are never static in the history of religion and changes came even to the afterlife. During Israel's exile in Babylon Persian ideas slipped into Judaism. One of them was that after death souls didn't end up as permanent residents in a dreary convalescent hospital in the Underworld. They either won entrance to the bliss of Paradise or they were condemned to the torment of Hell. This version of the afterlife never found full acceptance in Judaism, but it had its supporters in the first century CE. Jesus was one of them. Though he did not say much about it, he seemed to take the existence of Hell for granted. And the word he used for it gave it a new and terrifying twist.

Jesus said those who despised and damaged children would be cast into *Gehenna* 'into the fire that never shall be quenched'. In some old Hebrew writings Gehenna was the place where sinners would be punished after Judgment Day. A later tradition claimed that it was the name of the Jerusalem rubbish dump where garbage burned and smouldered continuously because they kept feeding it. It's impossible to know what Jesus intended by using it as a metaphor for unending punishment, but a furnace that never went out became a standard part of the equipment of Hell. By the time the Qur'an was written, six centuries later, those who were sentenced to everlasting punishment heard the furnace drawing in its breath as they approached it. And as they were being cast into the flames its Keeper asked them: 'Did there not come to you a Warner?'

The Qur'an was much more detailed in its description of Hell than the Christian scriptures. And it knew exactly what it was doing when it described it in such graphic detail. The message was that if people ignored the warnings of the Prophet they would not only be dragged into the flames of Hell, but as added torment boiling water would be poured on their heads. By the time of the Prophet the managers of the Inferno really had their act together and knew how to run an efficient and scarily effective system. Scaring people into religion has always been an effective tactic. The disadvantage Christianity confronted in its rivalry with Islam was that the Qur'an was much scarier than the New Testament. So Christianity decided it had to up its game. Perhaps the Church's holy book couldn't beat the Qur'an in the terror stakes, but it had a weapon in its arsenal that was not available to Muslims.

Unlike Islam, the Catholic Church had never been too bothered by the Second Commandment's prohibition of images. It believed that art in all its forms could be used to glorify God and get the Christian message across. So the Catholic Church became the greatest patron of artists the world has ever seen. It used music and architecture to celebrate and proclaim the faith. But above all other art forms, it loved making images. That meant that while Muslims could only describe Hell in words, Christians could *paint* it. And everyone knew a picture was worth a thousand words. So to make sure the message of Hell came through clear as well as loud, they painted it in sickening detail on the walls of churches. Here's an example.

There's a fifteenth-century church in the English town of Salisbury named after Thomas Becket. Becket was the Archbishop of Canterbury who was murdered in his cathedral on 29 December 1170 on the order of King Henry II. The church named in his honour in Salisbury is a gracious old building into which light flows kindly. But looming at you from the wall of the chancel arch as you walk down the central aisle is a medieval 'doom' painting. *Doom* in Anglo Saxon meant Judgment Day, Doomsday, when the dead would be called from their graves to hear God's verdict on their lives. Doom paintings were designed to scare people. This one must have been very effective.

Painted in 1475, it shows Christ on the seat of judgment. On his right the virtuous are being sent up to Heaven where they are met by welcoming angels. But on his left sinners are being sent down to Hell, where demons are dragging them to the dragon's mouth of the flaming pit. The people who first gazed at that painting would have taken it literally. Their universe was like a three-decker cake, with Heaven on top, Earth in the middle and Hell below. When you died you went 'up' to Heaven or 'down' to Hell, which was thought to be at the core of the earth itself. When volcanoes spewed out burning lava it was believed that 'Hell had opened her mouth' to give sinners a taste of what was waiting for them down below.

Christianity not only painted Hell on the walls of its churches, its preachers used their imagination to describe its terrors in their sermons. In his autobiographical novel, *A Portrait of the Artist as a Young Man*, Irish writer James Joyce recorded a sermon he heard as a boy when the preacher told his teenage audience that the sulphurous brimstone that burned in hell was designed, like the flames of Gehenna, to last for ever. Earthly fire, roared the preacher, destroyed as it burned. The more intense the heat the shorter would be its duration. But the fire of hell *preserved* those it burned so that their pain *never ceased!*

It is the thought of the endlessness of the pain in Hell that catches in the throat even if you don't believe in it. To be able to dream up such an idea! Humans have done terrible things to each other down the centuries. But even the grimmest of punishments had to come to an end at some point, if it was only in the death of the victim. The evil genius of Hell was that its pain never ended. Its prisoners spent eternity in a *now* with no *then* to look forward to. On the Salisbury doom painting the artist had included a scroll with a Latin motto – *Nulla in redemptio*, there is no redemption. A century before the unknown artist painted those words on the walls of Saint Thomas's in Salisbury an Italian poet called Dante wrote a famous poem about what he called the *Inferno*. And on the gate of his Hell he inscribed the warning: 'abandon hope all ye who enter here'.

It's the same message. Hell is without end and without hope, the grimmest prospect that can ever face a human being. It is worth noting that St Thomas Aquinas, the Catholic Church's greatest theologian – and a kindly man as well – said that an added attraction of Heaven was that it had a convenient balcony from which its citizens could watch the torments of the damned down below: 'In order that the bliss of the saints may be more delightful for them . . . it is given to them to see perfectly the punishment of the damned.' So Hell was agony for the damned and bliss for the redeemed.

So far, so horrifying. But religion can be good at recognising and modifying its more extreme teachings. We saw Muslim scholars suggesting that the doctrine of predestination in the Qur'an was incompatible with the mercy of Allah. Something like this happened with Hell in the Catholic Church. Was there not perhaps a middle way for those who were neither good enough to enter Heaven at death nor bad enough to be thrown into Hell? Wouldn't it be great if we could set up a training centre where sinners might be intensively prepared for resitting the examination for Heaven?

The need was acknowledged and in the twelfth century such a place was officially established. It was called Purgatory. The difference between Hell and Purgatory was that Purgatory had an exit. Saint Thomas Aquinas was the great authority on how it worked. He explained that if people died before paying the penalty for their sins, they got a second chance in Purgatory. The great thing about Purgatory was that it was a place of hope. Sure, it was also a place of pain, but those who endured it knew it wouldn't last forever and after they had done their time the gates of Heaven would open for them.

The establishment of Purgatory was an act of mercy that took some of the fear out of dying. But the Church had a way of corrupting even its own kindnesses. That's what happened here. The Church turned Purgatory into a money-making racket that was so outrageous it tore the Catholic Church apart. In the next chapter we'll begin to explore how it happened.

CHAPTER 26

Vicar of Christ

In the thousand years after the establishment of Christianity as the official religion of the Roman Empire by Constantine in the fourth century, the Church grew from a persecuted sect waiting for the return of Christ to become the largest and most powerful institution on the planet. Mighty in worldly as well as in spiritual power, it claimed to unite heaven and earth in a seamless unity. A magnificent institution, splendid in its vices as well as in its virtues, it bestrode the earth, humbling monarchs and commanding armies. And though it was light years away from the crucified prophet it claimed to follow, Jesus remained in the background as a troubling presence whose influence over it was never extinguished.

At the height of its powers in the thirteenth and fourteenth centuries the Catholic Church learned the single most important lesson a religion must master if it is to keep afloat on the rough seas of history. As we have seen, by their very nature religions are easily fragmented. It doesn't take a lot to shatter them. The death of one man can do it. As can the dispute over a vowel in a single word.

The Catholic Church decided that the best way to avoid these frac-
tures was to concentrate its power in a single individual and build
structures around him that would make his authority stick.

It achieved this by creating a dedicated order of priests to run
the lower levels of its vast organisation. Catholic priests were not
allowed to marry and develop the kind of human loyalties that
might compete with their spiritual role. The Church was to be their
family. In return for the personal sacrifice this required of them
they were accorded huge prestige and a special, sacred status. This
was given through a spiritual mechanism called the *apostolic
succession*. Like imams in the Shia version of Islam, Catholic clergy
received their authority not from a human but from a divine
source. This is how it worked.

Jesus had called twelve apostles to help him in his mission. And
he had ordained them to their work by laying his hands on their
heads. Using the same method, the apostles handed on their
authority to those who followed them. The Catholic Church
claimed that this chain of succession by the laying on of hands had
never been broken. It was a great pipeline that ran unbroken
through history. Break the line of succession or go to a different
supplier and you lost the authority of Jesus. Catholic bishops and
the priests and deacons they ordained thus became a special caste,
separated from ordinary human beings. To injure or insult a priest
was a special kind of offence. It was a sacrilege, a crime against
God. And it was punished accordingly.

Important as the creation of this elite caste was to the unity of
the Catholic Church, the real clincher in the system was how it
came to concentrate absolute power in a single figure, the Bishop
of Rome. By the time the process was complete the Bishop of Rome
was the most powerful man on earth. His words had authority not
only over life on earth but over the life to come after death. He
could imprison you on earth or ban you from heaven with equal
ease. When it was at its zenith the power of the Bishop of Rome
was immense. But it had taken centuries to achieve. To understand
how it came about we need to go back to the Emperor Constantine
in the fourth century.

It's wrong to assume that Rome was always the operational centre of the Roman Empire. It was, until the year 330 when Constantine decided to establish his imperial offices at the eastern end of the empire. He built a fabulous city called Constantinople, naming it after himself. Today we know it as Istanbul in Turkey. Its foundation set a couple of changes in motion. Constantinople became the most important city in the empire and a large part of its grandeur attached itself to the local bishop. Bishops of cities like Rome and Constantinople became powerful figures who assumed authority over the bishops of less important places.

In the cities of the Eastern Empire top bishops began to call themselves *patriarchs*, from the Greek for father. In the West they called themselves *popes*, from the Latin for father. Behind the different languages they used, other more profound disagreements had developed. They were still in theory one Church but they were beginning to pull apart. Like many quarrels in history, the divorce when it came was over who was in charge. Jesus had scolded his apostles for arguing over which of them would be the greatest when his kingdom would be established on earth. A similar dispute broke out between the Bishop of Constantinople and the Bishop of Rome. Which was greater, Eastern patriarch or Western pope? And Jesus wasn't around to referee it.

In reality the spiritual power was flowing to Rome. The fact that the Emperor was no longer resident in Rome meant that the pope became the unrivalled source of authority in the old capital. Whereas, in Constantinople the patriarch always had the emperor outshining him and breathing down his neck. In 1054 the smouldering rivalry between the two sides blazed into what became known as the Great Schism. Two distinct versions of Christianity emerged: the Orthodox Church in the East and the Catholic Church in the West with its pope in Rome. The division continues to this day, each side with its own style and culture. Orthodox clergy usually have beards; Catholic clergy usually don't. Orthodox priests may marry; Catholic priests may not. But behind these superficial differences there lay a profound disagreement over the source of the supreme authority the pope of Rome had assumed.

On the surface it could have been seen as an ordinary power grab. After all, power is the most addictive drug known and people will go to great lengths to gain and keep it. But disputants in religious power struggles are always careful to cover their ambition in sacred garments. It's never about human politics. It's always about obedience to God. We saw it in the struggle between Shia and Sunni in Islam. The Shia cloaked their power grab in a spiritual theory related to descent from the Prophet. The Pope of Rome had a similar card up his sleeve. His claim to precedence wasn't just that Rome was historically the most important city in the Empire. There was more to it than that. Christ himself had planned it that way! Here's how the argument went.

When Jesus called the twelve apostles he had given the top spot to Peter. And to make sure the others were in no doubt about Peter's position he had even given him a nickname. His real name, his Jewish name, was Simon. But Jesus had called him his Rock, *Petros* in Greek, *Petra* in Latin. 'You used to be called Simon', Jesus said, 'but from now on you'll be called Simon *Peter*, Simon the Rock. On you I will build my community.' And that wasn't all.

Do you remember where Peter died? It was in Rome during the first persecution of Christians in 65 CE. Since Peter was in Rome when he was executed, he must have been the first Bishop of Rome. Since he was the chief of the apostles you could argue that those who followed him as bishops of Rome inherited his status. Therefore the Bishop of Rome, Peter's successor, must be the chief of all bishops, Christ's vicar – or representative – on earth. The Church in the East didn't buy it. It was stretching it to say Peter had been the first Bishop of Rome. In his time Christians hadn't expected to be around for long. They'd been told Jesus Christ would be back soon. Why would they have bothered to set up an organisation that would soon disappear like everything else?

The Eastern Church had history on its side of the argument. The way the Church was organised owed more to Constantine than to Jesus Christ. So they refused to accept the Pope's authority over them and took themselves off. That left the Pope of Rome top man in the Western Church. But he wasn't finished yet in accumulating power. To understand the next development we have to go back to those souls trudging their way through Purgatory.

Remember: to the religious mind of the time this life was only a preparation for the everlasting life to come. How you would spend it depended on how you had behaved on earth. Sin could land you in Hell – or Purgatory if you got a break. That's why receiving forgiveness for your sins before you died was such a big deal. Some people tried to play the long game. They delayed getting baptised and having their sins washed away until just before they died. That meant they could have their fun down here while guaranteeing reasonably comfortable accommodation in the world to come. That's what Constantine himself had done. He'd delayed his baptism until he was near death. He judged it finely but made it in time.

You only have to reflect on this for a second to realise that if you had the ability to forgive people their sins and guarantee them a place in Heaven it would give you colossal power over them. The Pope believed he had that authority. Jesus had given it to Peter and he was Peter's successor. In the twelfth century the popes started to use this power in a way that would ultimately cause the Catholic rock to split apart. And it was Islam that was to blame.

When we looked at the history of Islam we noticed its dramatic spread in the southern and eastern regions of the Roman Empire after the Prophet's death. One of the areas it had conquered was Palestine. So the holy city of Jerusalem, sacred to Jews and Christians, landed in Muslim hands. Of course, Muslims also revered Jerusalem. It was their holy city too. Was not the Prophet the divinely appointed successor of Abraham, Moses and Jesus?

That's not how the Pope saw it. To him Muslim possession of Christianity's holy city was an affront. So he decided to take it back. A campaign was mounted to persuade Christian warriors from Europe to go to Jerusalem and win it back for the Catholic Church. Those who responded to the challenge and rode off to battle were called Crusaders, a word that meant marked with the cross. Like Constantine, who had fought his rival at the Milvian Bridge near Rome behind a banner of the cross, the Crusaders used the symbol of the crucified Jesus to lead them in battle against the Muslims who ruled Palestine.

Pope Urban II sent off the First Crusade in 1095. There were seven more in the following two centuries. Though Jerusalem was won back for a time, the crusades caused as much damage to the Christians of the Eastern Church as they did to Muslims. They left an indelible stain on Catholic history. But here's the fateful development. As an incentive to get men to go on crusade the Pope offered them the forgiveness of *all* their sins. The technical word for the deal was an *indulgence*, from the Latin for concession. There was a spiritual logic in the offer. After all, riding or marching hundreds of miles from home and enduring the danger of battle might be thought of as a payback for bad behaviour, like a fine or community service imposed by justice systems today.

It was when a future Pope decided that indulgences could become a nice little money spinner for a pet building project that trouble started for the Church. As we'll see in the next few chapters.

CHAPTER 27

Protest

On a spring morning in the year 1517 a preacher got up on his soapbox in the square of Jüterbog in Germany and began to bellow at the audience that had gathered to hear him. What he said was the spark to the dynamite that blew Christendom apart.

Roll up! Roll up! This is your day of grace, my friends. This is the day you get out of jail. All you need is this little letter. This little letter in my hand only costs a shilling but it will save you years of misery in purgatory.

You are all faithful Catholics. You know sin has to be punished. Sin has to be paid for! Confess all you like, it won't make any difference. Those sins have to be paid for in purgatory! Seven years for every mortal sin.

How many mortal sins do you commit in a year? How many mortal sins do you commit in a lifetime? Add them up. Before you know it you've clocked up hundreds of years in purgatory. Think about it!

But one of these little letters will get you off. A shilling in this box and you'll be released from all that misery. And listen to this. This letter will get you time off purgatory not only for the sins you've already committed but for the sins you haven't got round to yet! What a bargain!

What's in the letter? It's an indulgence. And it comes from our Holy Father the Pope himself. The Pope has sent me here to tell you that if you buy an indulgence now, when you die the gate of Hell will be bolted shut but the door of Heaven will open wide for you.

And the offer is not just for the living. It's for the dead as well! Think about your relatives and friends stuck in Purgatory. Think of the years that stretch ahead of them. On and on they go. Painful years, punishing years! But buy one of these indulgences and your relatives will be lifted out of Purgatory and in the blink of an eye they'll be in Heaven!

And here's another thing. This indulgence will not only do you and your loved ones a favour, it will do the Holy Catholic Church a favour. The great church in Rome where the bodies of Saint Peter and Saint Paul are buried is in a bad way. Our Holy Father Pope Leo wants to build a church that will humble the world with its beauty and magnificence. You can help to build it! Your shilling will buy a stone, and stone by stone the new Saint Peter's will rise to stun the world with its glory.

Roll up! Roll up! Indulgences for sale a shilling apiece!

The preacher's name was Johann Tetzel and he belonged to a branch of the Church's special forces called the Order of Preachers, or Dominicans. He was fifty-two years old, a tough man, built like a bull. And in his time he'd done some rough work for the Church.

Two centuries before Tetzel's sermon in the square in Jüterbog, Pope Gregory IX had set up an order of enforcers called the Inquisition. Its agents or inquisitors were commissioned to root out false teaching in the Church by any means, including torture. Their most effective tool was the rack, a wooden frame with two ropes fixed to the bottom and another two tied to a handle at the top. The accused's arms and legs were bound to the ropes and the torturer turned the handle till their bones dislocated with an ugly crack. If that didn't get the confession he wanted, he kept turning till the victim's arms were torn from the body. It was a world away from loving your enemies and blessing those who cursed you; an example of how religion's preoccupation with life after death so often made it an enemy of life before death.

Tetzel had been a member of the Inquisition. It was his success as a persuader that had prompted the Archbishop of Mainz to make him his chief sales director for indulgences. The Archbishop was in trouble. His large diocese was in debt. And on top of that the Pope was chasing him for a large contribution to the campaign for the rebuilding of Saint Peter's in Rome. That's when the Archbishop had a brainwave. Why not do a deal with Rome? Get the Pope to license Tetzel the Persuader as his official salesman for indulgences, on condition that half the money raised could be kept for the Archdiocese of Mainz, the other half going to Rome. It would be a win–win for both the embattled Archbishop and the Pope who was putting the squeeze on him. The deal was struck. That's what brought Tetzel and his circus to Jüterbog that April morning in 1517. And the money soon started rolling in.

But months after Tetzel's sales pitch in Jüterbog another thick-set German priest ruined the deal. Outraged at the idea that Christians could buy their way into Heaven, he nailed onto the door of the church in the neighbouring city of Wittenberg a document in Latin denouncing the sale of indulgences as un-Christian. Within weeks it had been translated into German as well as other European languages. By the end of November 1517 it was the talk of Europe. In Rome Pope Leo dismissed it with a joke. Another drunk German, he purred. He'll change his mind when he sobers up.

The 'drunk German' was a dedicated monk called Martin Luther. And he never did change his mind. It was the Pope who had to change his. Amusement turned to anger when he was told that as a result of the monk's document the sale of indulgences had fallen and very little money was coming in. His scheme to rebuild Saint Peter's was at risk. So Leo issued an order called a papal bull removing Martin Luther from the priesthood and banning all his writings. When Luther received his copy he burned it in public.

But he burned more than a papal bull that day. He burned the bridges that bound him to the Catholic Church and started an international revolt described by historians as the Reformation. By the time it had run its course Christian Europe was in fragments.

Martin Luther had been born in Eisleben on 10 November 1483, the son of Hans and Margarethe Luther. Though poor and with seven children to feed, Martin's parents were determined to give their clever son a good education. He attended the University of Erfurt and in 1505 he became a monk in the famous Augustinian order. He was ordained a priest two years later and in 1512 he began teaching at the University of Wittenberg. He was marked out for early promotion, and in 1510 his superiors sent him to Rome to negotiate business on behalf of the order. After the sombre pace of life in Wittenberg, Luther was appalled by the frivolity and corruption he encountered in the Eternal City. But he came back to Wittenberg worried about more that the state of the great Roman Catholic Church. He was anxious about his own soul and whether the Church was any longer capable of saving it from Hell. The indulgences racket and other corruptions hadn't helped. But the main source of his unease wasn't the Church. It was his discovery of the Bible.

Not that the Bible had ever been lost. Selections from it were read in Latin every day at Mass. But by this time the Catholic Church used the Bible mainly to back up its own authority. It spoke of the Christ who had lived long ago in the Holy Land – the same Holy Land it had sent the crusaders to rescue from the Muslims – but what mattered was that the Pope was now Christ's vicar on earth. Anything important in the Bible had been assumed into the Pope. It was the Pope who held the keys to Heaven or Hell, not old words in a book few could read because it was written in Latin. And few of the priests who read it at Mass understood it either. It was a recitation like the recitation of the Qur'an: powerful even if you didn't understand it.

But by the time of Luther there were people who were able to read and understand the Bible. And not just in the Latin it had been translated into a thousand years before. Scholars like Luther were reading the Old Testament in the original Hebrew and the New Testament in the original Greek. And its message began to scare them. *This* was God's word, they realised, not the words that came from the mouth of the Pope. The Bible was good news if you got it right but very bad news if you got it wrong. Luther began to fear that the Catholic Church had got it wrong, terribly wrong.

The Bible was the story of a people who had been chosen by God. It was a marriage. God had wed himself to Israel. Tragically, she had been unfaithful. And by the time of Jesus God had divorced Israel, his faithless bride, and chosen a new one, the Christian Church. Was history repeating itself? Was the Catholic Church any longer the pure Bride of Christ? Or had she become an unfaithful wife who ran after worldly success and the pleasures it bought?

The story of the broken covenant between Israel and God is a key that unlocks the meaning of the Reformation. To feel its force we have to recall the momentous claim that the Christian Church made for itself. It offered men and women the good news of eternal bliss or the bad news of eternal woe. If they were faithful to their covenant with God a glorious future awaited them in Heaven. But the price of infidelity was the kind of eternal torment graphically depicted in that doom painting in Saint Thomas's in Salisbury.

How to be saved was the obsession that burned in the mind of Martin Luther. As he read the letters of Saint Paul, another Christian obsessive, he had a revelation, a moment of insight into God. He would not be saved by endless prayers and pilgrimages. Or by indulgences signed by the Pope himself. They would turn his relationship with God into a business transaction, something he could buy. He knew it was impossible to buy God's love. Then it hit him. He couldn't buy God's love but he didn't need to *because God gave it freely!* It was God's *love* that would save him. Not a shoddy deal brokered by the Church. He should trust in that love, trust in God alone, not in the Church or the Pope or any other human agency.

Though he could not have realised the impact it would have on the centuries to come, that event in Luther's mind was a turning point in the human story. It unleashed two forces that would change history forever: the Bible and free individuals standing face to face before their God. Its immediate effect was the shattering of the unity of the once impregnable Catholic Church. The Protestant Reformation was off and running. In the following chapters we'll examine the consequences.

CHAPTER 28

The Big Split

The revelation that came to Martin Luther telling him he would be saved not by performing religious duties or buying indulgences but only by God's love for him, was an idea that was never fully taken up by Christianity. Luther himself didn't recognise its revolutionary meaning. Nor did he always live up to it in his dealings with others. But it had come to him. And it was now out there.

The technical term scholars gave to Luther's insight itself tells a story. They called it *justification by faith*. The clue lies in that word 'justification'. Forget the sense it has nowadays of someone trying to explain away something they're ashamed of or are being challenged about. Think instead of someone up before a judge for a criminal act. They're guilty and they know it. And they know the judge knows it. Yet to their amazement the judge *justifies* them, pronounces them guiltless and sets them free.

Luther had glimpsed a different way of understanding humanity's relationship with God. The impression religion had given people was that God was out to get them. They were being marked for an examination they had never seen the questions for. That's why the different religions were so competitive with each other. Only they knew the questions on the paper. Only they could coach you for the test you were registered for at birth when you knew nothing about anything. But Luther had caught sight of a different way of seeing God. It was love he saw, a love that offered itself to the world without condition or requirement. If true, it meant humans could live freely and happily without constantly looking over their shoulders at the avenging god who was out to get them.

To understand how radical was Luther's flash of insight we have to remember how religions had traditionally operated. There were differences between them, but what they had in common could be captured in the word 'required'. Religions were there to save men and women from a terrible fate. But to be saved they were required to believe certain doctrines and perform certain tasks. Religion was what the Romans called a *quid pro quo* or one thing for another. Believe this, perform that, and this will be the result. Sometimes the requirement was negative. Don't believe this! Don't do that! If you accepted the idea of the demanding god on which it was grounded it made sense. Religion was a transaction, a deal, an insurance policy. That's certainly what an indulgence was. Buy it and your future was protected. And it was how a lot of human interactions worked, not just religion. To get something out you had to put something in. It was a business.

That hadn't been how Jesus had seen humanity's relationship with God. But the things he'd said were so puzzling, those who ran the Church never tried to follow them. He told a story about the owner of a vineyard who gave everyone the same pay at the end of the day, no matter how long they'd worked. God's relationship with humanity was not based on employment law, he said. It was one-to-one, bespoke, tailored to the particular needs of the individual. In an even more upsetting parable a young man demanded his inheritance from his father and wasted it all in riotous living. Then he was welcomed home by his father without a word of censure. God's like that, Jesus said. No matter how we behave, he won't stop loving us. Try to love like that yourselves!

It was crazy! To run the world that way would cause chaos in its systems and institutions, including religion. Yet it was the possibility of a Church motivated by love that Luther had glimpsed that night in his study in Wittenberg. As his hero Paul had put it, love bore all things and endured all things. God's love for his children could not be defeated by anything, including their own lawless acts. However guilty they were, God went on loving them. It was love that would save them, not fear and the deals it generated.

But the Church had allowed a religion of divine kindness to be transformed into a religion of human cruelty. That's what Constantine had done when he had slaughtered his enemies under the banner of the Cross of Jesus. That's what the crusaders had done when they went off to kill Muslims in the Holy Land. And that's what the Inquisition had done when it tore the arms off heretics on the rack. They all thought it was fine to make people submit to their version of God. And that was because their version of God was just a version of themselves.

Luther had seen in a flash how wrong all that was. And it gave him courage to stand against the Catholic Church's power and greed and call for something new. So the Protestant religion was born. As its name suggests, Protestantism defined itself more by what it was against than by what it was for. But its opposition to the cruelty of power brought something precious into European history. And it became a force that would in time challenge political as well as religious tyranny.

Because of the way society was ordered at the time, the Protestant movement couldn't get very far without the approval and support of local rulers. Europe was not a democracy. So the reformed churches needed the backing of the ruling kings and dukes if they were to establish themselves. Alliances with the rulers were formed and new churches emerged. But they didn't all see things the same way or believe in the same things. So the Big Split from Rome was followed by smaller splits among Protestants who disagreed with each other over what the new purified Church should look like. The genius of Protestantism was also its greatest weakness: its inability to compromise with anything it disapproved of.

The genius of the Roman Church had been its resistance to division. Its single-mindedness was the glue that had bound different peoples in different places into one faith. Even the use of Latin in the Mass had been unifying. Only the educated understood it and there were never many of them around, even among the clergy. So the people who went to Mass across Europe were one in their ignorance of what was being said at the altar. But they were also one in their participation in a sacred mystery that was the same everywhere. At the Reformation that unity was lost forever, except in the Catholic Church itself.

After the convulsions of the Reformation the Catholic Church responded with its own reform movement, known as the Counter-Reformation. Pope Paul III convened a council at Trent in Italy that sat between 1545 and 1563. As expected, it denounced the writings of Martin Luther but it also criticised the abuses in the Church that had prompted them. The Church that liked to call itself the Barque of Saint Peter, after the apostle it liked to call the First Pope, had survived the storm that had threatened to capsize it. It sailed on into history, buffeted by the occasional wind but never again seriously threatened.

The same could not be said of the Protestant Churches. If we can stick to the nautical metaphor a moment longer, from a few large ships flying under national flags, Protestantism soon multiplied into fleets of competing vessels, some of them not much bigger than a canoe. Two factors contributed to this multiplication effect. And the main one was the Bible. Once you liberate a book from the control of a single authority it becomes subject to many interpretations, especially if it is believed to have been inspired by God. Luther had discovered justification by faith in the Bible. But there was a lot more to be found there, much of it contradictory. The Bible, after all, was a library of books written and rewritten over the centuries by many unknown authors. There was something for everyone there, depending on the needs and fears that drove them. Some of the new Protestant Churches found themselves more inspired by the Old Testament than by the New. We'll look at the effect that had on the way the Reformation worked out in different nations. We'll also see how the ancient longing for an absolute authority in religion shifted from an infallible pope to an infallible Bible.

The other cause of division among Protestants was the way the Reformation had liberated individuals. Traditional religion hadn't given much freedom of choice to ordinary believers. They had to do what they were told by the priests and bishops who ran the Church. By affirming the conscience of individuals and their right to a personal relationship with God, the Reformation destroyed that kind of authoritarianism. It rejected the idea that individuals had to approach God through officially approved experts. It believed in the priesthood of all believers, not just in those who had been ordained into the apostolic succession. That's why Protestantism was hard to organise into a single institution. There were always rebels who challenged the people who had taken charge. And if they were not listened to they went off and started their own Church.

But the biggest failure of the Churches of the Reformation was that they never challenged the way Constantine had corrupted Christianity into using violence against its opponents. Luther had had his flash of insight into the way of love, but the heavens had closed their doors again and in dealing with opponents Luther was as ruthless as the worst of them. He was never reluctant to put the boot in when his authority was challenged.

And that is exactly what he did when the peasants of Germany, stimulated by the Reformation's challenge to the power of the Church, wondered why they couldn't be liberated from the power landowners had over their lives. They weren't quite slaves but they were close to it. They were serfs, agricultural labourers with no rights and no way of ever lifting themselves out of poverty. They were there to work themselves to death for the nobles in their grand houses and palaces. The Church had blessed the arrangement as ordained by God. 'The rich man in his castle, the poor man at his gate, God made them high or lowly, and ordered their estate', as a popular hymn would later express it. The peasants didn't see it that way. And the Reformation had given them hope.

If the Church could change, why couldn't society? If Martin Luther could overturn the might of the Roman Church, why couldn't they overthrow the power of German landowners?

Their rebellion, called the Peasants' Revolt, lasted only a year, from 1524 to 1525. With the angry and enthusiastic support of Luther, the authorities brutally suppressed the uprising and a hundred thousand were killed during the rebellion. When it was over, vigilante gangs roamed the countryside beating up the peasants who were left and burning them out of their hovels. It was another example of the way religion's obsession with getting people into Heaven made it uninterested in finding better ways to help them get along on earth. Luther's involvement in the suppression of the Peasants' Revolt might be described as the first Protestant Crusade. There would be others, usually Protestant against Protestant. Everything had changed. Yet everything had stayed the same.

By the end of the sixteenth century, with the exception of Ireland, Northern Europe was almost completely Protestant. The new churches took different forms and they were often in violent disagreement with each other. But Europe wasn't the only continent going through a religious crisis. India was having one as well. So before crossing the Channel to see what happened when the Reformation hit England and Scotland, we'll do another zigzag to see what was going on in India.

CHAPTER 29

Nanak's Reformation

Martin Luther wouldn't have liked him and the feeling would have been mutual, but he had much in common with Guru Nanak, the founder of the Sikh religion. They lived during the same turbulent era. Nanak was born in 1469, Luther in 1483. Nanak died in 1539, Luther seven years later in 1546. They would never have heard of each other and they lived four thousand miles apart, Nanak in India, Luther in Germany. But each was a reformer of the religion he had been born into. Worlds apart in how they lived and what they believed, they remind us how religions have a tendency to split in their search for truth and purity.

A Sikh is a disciple or follower of the Guru Nanak and the nine gurus who succeeded him. Though Nanak was the founder of Sikhism, the faith he conceived did not achieve its final form until 1708 on the death of the tenth and last guru. A *guru* is a teacher who makes God's meaning clear and God's presence real. Before he died Guru Nanak appointed Guru Angad to follow him. And before Guru Angad died in 1552 he appointed Guru Amar Das as his successor. In this way the apostolic succession of the gurus of

Sikhism was handed on until it reached its tenth Guru, Gobind Singh, in 1676.

Then something interesting happened. Guru Gobind Singh decided not to appoint a successor. From now on, he declared, the guru who represented God within the Sikh community would exist in two different but related ways. First, the Sikh holy book would be the guru. Called the *Guru Granth Sahib*, it would command the central place in a Sikh temple or *gurdwara* (meaning gateway to the guru) as the symbol of God's presence in their midst.

The second mode of the Guru would be the community of believers who had been initiated into the Sikh religion, called the *Guru Khalsa Panth* or guru of the pure way. Like some of the Churches that emerged in Christianity at the Reformation, Sikhs did not believe in the need for a priests' union to supervise their faith. The faithful had no need of intermediaries between themselves and God. All believers were equal in God's sight. So it might help to think of Sikhs as the Protestants of Indian religion and to see the guru of the pure way as the priesthood of all believers beloved of Christianity's reformers. There are other aspects of Sikhism that can be read as a form of Indian Protestantism, but let us go back now to Nanak, Sikhism's first guru, to see how it all started.

Nanak was born in the Punjab in north-west India to Hindu parents of the merchant caste. It had been a long time since Hinduism was the dominant religion of India. Islam had taken over. Muslim traders had first arrived in India in the eighth century CE and they brought their faith with them. As always, India was hospitable to religion in any of its forms and Islam took root in the subcontinent among all the other systems. Then in the tenth century Muslims from neighbouring Afghanistan started to make raids into the Punjab. At the time they seemed more interested in carrying off loot than in imposing their faith, but they must have been appalled by the polytheism they encountered.

Muslim invasions continued and by the time Nanak was born in the fifteenth century the great Mughal Empire had begun to take control of India. The Mughals were originally from Mongolia in Central Asia, and by the time they arrived in India they had converted to Islam. When Nanak was a boy the Emperor of India was a Muslim. But a touch of Hindu universalism had rubbed off on the new rulers and the Mughal Empire was tolerant of different faiths. So Nanak, intensely committed to the spiritual quest, had a choice to make. Was it to be Hinduism or Islam?

He decided to go on pilgrimage to the holy sites of both religions in search of inspiration. It is said he got as far west as Mecca in Arabia. By the time he returned to the Punjab at the end of his travels he had decided that neither Hinduism nor Islam was the path he was searching for. After a mystical encounter with God, he proclaimed a different way. But when we examine what was revealed to him we can see that, though it had its own character, it also contained elements of the two religions it replaced. Like Muhammad and the leaders of the Protestant Reformation, Nanak hated showy religion. He was a monotheist with a profound contempt for the merchants of idolatry. He had seen how easy it was for religion to become a racket with spiritual conmen setting themselves up as God's sales reps. Nanak knew God was already in the hearts of ordinary women and men. God didn't need to work through agents. That's why Nanak disliked the kind of services that required professional priests to perform them.

In that opinion he was more Islamic than Hindu. But he was Hindu in his sympathy for the soul's longing to be rescued from its migratory wandering through life after life on earth. Belief in karma and reincarnation are the most distinctive of the Hindu doctrines and Nanak accepted them. God had told him that he himself had been released from the cycle of endless return. And it was to show them how they too might achieve salvation from the round of rebirths that he had been sent as a guru to his people. In one of the stories describing his spiritual experience, Nanak's mission was described like this. The Almighty said to him:

I release you from the cycle of birth, death and rebirth; he that sets his eyes on you with faith shall be saved. He that hears your words with conviction will be saved ... I grant you salvation. Nanak, go back to the evil world and teach men and women to pray, to give in charity and live cleanly. Do good to the world and redeem it in the age of sin.

So far we might decide that all Nanak had done was to take bits from Hinduism and Islam and repackage them. But what he did next was radical and distinctive – and still is. He got people eating together. That may not sound new or important, but in the history of religion it was revolutionary. In religious communities believers had to learn which people they were permitted or forbidden to eat with. There was even a technical name for it: *commensality*, meaning groups they were allowed to sit at table with. And most of the energy went into saying whom they couldn't eat with. That's because the idea of purity runs deep in the religious psyche, the belief that there are unclean foods and unclean people. If you touch them you make yourself disgusting to God and in need of purification. It's strongest in countries that practise caste or racial separation. It was there in the Hindu caste system where even the shadow of an untouchable falling over a Brahmin's lunch rendered it unclean, and it had to be thrown away.

Hinduism was not the only religion that practised this kind of discrimination. It was in Judaism as well. There were unclean races as well as unclean foods. One of the charges made against Jesus was that he ignored these taboos. He not only spoke to sinners, he ate with them! The Church that claimed to follow in his way soon found reasons for not following his example. The eating taboo is still at work in Christianity. The main service of Christian worship is a ritualised meal called the Lord's Supper or Holy Communion or Mass. It is based on the last meal Jesus had with his disciples on the night before he died, when he told them to go on doing it in remembrance of him. Christians have celebrated it ever since. But they won't eat it with everyone. Roman Catholics won't eat it with Protestants. There are Protestants who won't eat it with other Protestants or anyone outside the purity of their own circle. And many Christians believe that if you've sinned you shouldn't be allowed to eat it at all. It's like being sent to bed without supper as a punishment for misbehaving.

Nanak hated all these taboos. He saw how they built walls of separation between people in the name of the God who loved them all equally. His response was brilliantly simple. He introduced the custom of the *langar* or communal meal in the Sikh community. It was open to all castes. And it was free of those ritual embellishments priests love to embroider onto human activities. It was an ordinary meal! They ate it together like a family. In a Sikh gurdwara the kitchen is as holy as any other part of the building. Food is cooked and shared to celebrate the equality of all, no matter their caste, creed, race or gender. That's why the gurdwara has four doors at the points of the compass to symbolise that it is open to all comers. All the gurus who followed Nanak emphasised the importance of the langar in the Sikh faith. The third guru, Amar Das, even insisted that anyone who wanted to meet him, from the lowliest peasant to the Emperor of India himself, had first to eat a meal with him in the langar.

Each of the nine gurus who followed Nanak confirmed and adapted his vision to the needs of their day, but it was the tenth guru who gave Sikhism the dramatic identity that characterises it to this day. Mughal India might have been relatively tolerant, but it was far from being an open society and Sikhs had to protect themselves against Islamic disapproval. The sixth guru Hargobind (1595–1644) established a Sikh army to protect his community. But it was the tenth guru Gobind Singh (1666–1708) who gave Sikhism its edge. He encouraged his people to establish a fortified town and undertake military training – a reminder of how new religions usually have to protect themselves from persecution by the group they have abandoned. The Sikhs became legendary soldiers and adopted a martial style that still marks them today.

Sikhism has five principal features, referred to as the Five Ks. *Kesh* means uncut hair. Sikhs let their hair grow as a sign of their faith. Sikh men wear turbans to keep it under control. Women may wear either the turban or a scarf. *Khanga* is the comb symbolising purity which is fixed into the Sikh's long hair. *Kara* is a steel bracelet worn on the wrist as a symbol of the infinity of God. The *Kirpan* is a sword at the waist slung on a shoulder strap. It reminds

Sikhs not only of their military history but of their duty to fight for justice. *Kaccha* are soldiers' underpants, serving as a reminder of the need for self-discipline.

Unlike Christianity and Islam, Sikhism is not a proselytising religion. It is like Judaism in that it is as much a racial identity as it is a faith. And while it is happy to receive converts who want to join it, it does not chase across oceans in pursuit of them. This is because, unlike religions that see themselves as the only authorised route to salvation, Sikhs believe there are many paths to God. In this they show the generosity that characterised Indian spirituality, in contrast to the intolerance that has usually marked Christianity in the West. And that's a cue to leave India and head for Britain to see how the Reformation battles were raging there as the sixteenth century wore on.

CHAPTER 30

The Middle Way

When I was a student, one of my Church history lecturers was a man from Aberdeen who had a colourful way of speaking. When lecturing on the Reformation he used a metaphor I remember still. This is how he got us to think about the style of the different churches that emerged from the struggles of the sixteenth century.

'You have a wee son', he said, 'and he's been out playing with his pals. When he comes home at bedtime his face is filthy, covered in mud from the fields he's been roaming in all day. When you see the state he's in, what should you do? You have three options. You can send him to bed as he is and lay his dirty wee head down on your clean pillow case. You can chop off his head. That would get rid of the mud certainly, but you'd kill him in the process and no longer have a son. Or you can give him a bath and clean him up before tucking him in for the night.'

What was he getting at? He was exploring the idea of continuity with the past in the churches left standing after the Reformation. Three models were on offer, he said. There was continuity with no change; change with no continuity; or continuity with some change.

The Catholic Church was continuous with the Christianity that stretched back to the Apostles. By the sixteenth century it had acquired a dirty face like the wee boy, but beneath the grime it was what it had been from the beginning. It was Christian but unreformed.

But to the extreme reformers Catholicism was no longer Christian. The Pope didn't just have a dirty face, he was the Anti-Christ, someone who pretended to be a disciple of Christ but was in fact his enemy. It was as if a foreign agent had become president of a country in order to destroy it from within. Catholicism had gone over to the dark side. So its evil head had to be chopped off.

In the middle there were reformers who said all they were doing was washing the Church's face. They weren't getting rid of the Church – only of the grime that disfigured it. And of all the churches that emerged at the Reformation the one that most prized the middle ground and claimed it as her own was the Church in England. It said its dispute was not with the Catholic Church at all. It was with one of its bishops, the Bishop of Rome. What right had an Italian bishop to intervene in the affairs of another nation? His claim of authority over the whole world was not part of the Church's original identity. His grab for power had already caused the Great Schism between the Orthodox Church of the East and the Catholic Church of the West. He was up to his old tricks and if he wasn't careful there would be another Great Schism.

But there was another side to the story. And it had more to do with the marital difficulties of the King of England than with the ambitions of the Bishop of Rome. The king's name was Henry VIII, famous for his six wives, and to understand what it was all about we need to go back about forty years before his birth.

Henry was born on 28 June 1491, four years after the end of a series of wars that for thirty-seven years had torn England apart. The wars started in 1455 and raged until the Battle of Bosworth was won by Henry Tudor in 1485 and ended the conflict. He was then crowned as King Henry VII. Peace at last! But medieval kings could never take peace for granted. 'Uneasy lies the head that wears a crown', wrote William Shakespeare, the great English playwright and student of monarchy.

The future King Henry VIII would have grown up with stories of the struggles that had led his father to the throne of England. He would have learned how alert a king had to be to the tiniest threat to his throne. But happily, this was of little importance to him. He had an older brother Arthur who would become king when Henry VII died. The young Henry, clever and athletic, was left to study hard and play hard. But when he was ten all that changed. His brother Arthur died, leaving a widow, Catherine of Aragon, a Spanish princess. Henry was now heir to the throne his father had fought to secure and keep. And when Henry VII died in 1509 his seventeen-year-old son succeeded him as Henry VIII and reigned for the next thirty-eight years.

Our part of the story starts when, upon taking the throne of England, Henry decided to marry his brother Arthur's widow, Catherine of Aragon, who was five years his senior. It was an unusual thing to do because the Bible seemed to forbid it. The Old Testament book of Leviticus expressly prohibited a man from marrying his brother's widow: 'If a man shall take his brother's wife, it is an unclean thing: he hath uncovered his brother's nakedness' – and here comes the really bad news – 'they shall be childless'. In order to go ahead with the marriage Henry had to get a special dispensation from the Pope. He got it and married Catherine. It shows that at this time Henry was only too happy to accept that the Pope had authority in the realm of England.

Trouble started when Catherine did not produce a male heir to the throne. This was a genuine worry to Henry, as it would have been to any medieval king. Guaranteeing a male heir was all that was really expected of queens at the time. Catherine had failed at the task. She had given him a daughter, Mary, but no son. And it was sons that counted. Henry knew his Bible. In fact he was a bit of a theologian. He could read Latin and Greek. And he was a strong Catholic. He hated all the reformation talk that was coming out of Europe. A pamphlet he had written attacking Luther's theology had won him a special title from Pope Leo X as Defender of the Faith, a title the monarch of the United Kingdom claims to this day. If you look at a pound coin you'll see the letters FD after the Queen's name, standing for *Fidei Defensor*, Latin for Defender of the Faith.

So whatever else he was, Henry VIII was no Protestant. He didn't want a new Church in England. He wanted a wife who would bear him a son. The solution was simple. The Pope had given him a dispensation to marry Catherine in spite of what the Bible said. The fact that she couldn't give him a son proved that the Pope should never have given his consent in the first place. What did that Leviticus passage say? *They shall be childless.* Since daughters didn't count, Henry thought he *was* childless. The Pope should annul the marriage, that is, declare that it had never been valid.

It was a tough call for the Pope. If he said yes to the annulment he would offend Catherine's relative the Emperor of Spain. If he said no he would outrage the King of England. So he did nothing, hoping something would turn up to get him off the hook.

What turned up was another woman in Henry's life, Anne Boleyn, one of Queen Catherine's ladies in waiting. Convinced he had been cursed for marrying his deceased brother's wife, and having fallen in love with Anne, Henry secretly married her in 1533. And in 1534, having persuaded his advisers to dig out an example from history, he declared himself Supreme Governor of the Church in England. The first use he made of his new authority over the Church was to annul his marriage to Catherine. The split from Rome was complete.

The thing to notice is that the split was not caused by Protestants calling for a new Church but by the King of England calling for a new wife. There were Protestants in England, of course. One of them was the King's chief fixer, Thomas Cromwell, though it is unlikely that Henry knew about his sympathies. From this tangle of circumstances there emerged a Church of England that claimed to be both Catholic and Reformed, the same yet different. It kept the old order of bishops, priests and deacons and claimed to be still within the apostolic succession. It kept most of the old calendar of feasts and fasts in a new Book of Common Prayer that allowed the English to worship in a beautiful version of their own language. It wasn't a new Church or even a different kind of Church. It was the old Catholic Church with a shiny clean face.

That, anyway, was how it liked to describe itself. But its origins were far from shiny clean. It was royal politics rather than reformed theology that separated England from the old Catholic Church. But the English Reformation illustrates a side of religion we should think about: the way it becomes unavoidably intertwined with human politics. *Politics*, from the Greek word for city, is the short-hand term for the way human beings organise their public lives, with all their tensions and disagreements. Politics invades every-thing, from squabbles in a school playground right up to debates in the United Nations.

And from the beginning religion has been part of the political mix. We might even say that the relationship between God and humanity is itself a kind of politics, since it's about figuring out how one relates to the other. Religion has been part of earthly poli-tics since the beginning. There is obviously politics *within* religion, such as disagreements about who should run the religion and how they get selected to do it.

But the really dangerous stuff happens when religion becomes a weapon in disputes between rival political powers who claim God is on their side of whatever the argument is. That is why we have to see the Reformation as a movement in which it is impossible to separate religion from the politics of the time, particularly in England. For the safety of his kingdom Henry needed a divorce; and if the Pope wouldn't or couldn't give it to him then he would have to find someone who would. So he split from Rome. The Church of England was born. And compromised though its origins were, it did think of itself as a middle way between extremes. It was still the Catholic Church, but with a cleaner face.

Henry got his divorce but it didn't make him happy. Anne Boleyn did not produce a son for him either, though she did produce a daughter. So the curse continued. Henry had Anne executed on a trumped-up charge of adultery. Next he married Jane Seymour, who did give him the son he wanted, named

Edward. And when Henry died in 1547 the nine-year-old Edward succeeded him.

During Edward's short reign the reforms of the Church of England were consolidated. But when he died in 1553 he was succeeded by Catherine of Aragon's daughter Mary and the religious politics of England swung in the other direction. The Catholic Church was reinstated and Mary took her revenge on those who had made her mother's life miserable. She was an enthusiastic persecutor of Protestants, many of whom she had burned to death for their heresies, earning herself the nickname Bloody Mary.

Mary died in 1558 and the pendulum swung again. She was succeeded by Anne Boleyn's daughter Elizabeth, who reigned until 1601 and brought peace and stability to the realm. The irony is that the daughter Henry VIII had not wanted turned out to be one of the wisest monarchs England had ever known. She stabilised the state and completed the reformation of the Church. But she could be as ruthless as her father. In 1587 she had her cousin Mary Queen of Scots beheaded for conspiracy. It took three blows of the axe to remove Mary's head, a grim end to an unhappy life. To understand why that happened we must go north to Scotland where the Reformation had taken a very different turn.

CHAPTER 31

Beheading the Beast

Being a queen in medieval Europe was dangerous. Your role was to forge alliances between nations and bear children to men who probably didn't love you. That's how it had been for Catherine of Aragon, the first wife of Henry VIII. She at least died in her own bed. Henry's grand-niece Mary Queen of Scots died on an executioner's block, a victim of the religious conflicts of her age. She was born in Scotland in 1542 to King James V and his French wife Mary of Guise. Her losses began early. Her father died weeks after her birth and she became, technically, Queen of Scotland. When she was five she was sent to live in France where she was married at fifteen to fourteen-year-old Francis, heir to the throne.

Her father-in-law King Henry II of France became the father she'd never known. She studied hard. She loved animals, especially dogs. And she led a comfortable and protected life. Then the losses started again. Her father-in-law died in 1559. Her husband became King Francis II and she the Queen Consort. A year later her mother the Queen Regent of Scotland died, followed six months later by her husband Francis. At eighteen Mary was an orphan and a widow. The Catholic faith she had learned as a child sustained her in her sorrow. And she brought her faith with her when she was called back to Scotland to become its queen. But in the years she had been away Scotland had become Protestant. How would it respond to its Catholic queen?

She reached the land of her birth on 19 August 1561. As she prepared for her first night in her palace at the bottom of the Royal Mile in Edinburgh she heard singing outside her window. It wasn't a welcome home party serenading her with some of Scotland's old songs. It was a group of protesters warning her with some of Scotland's new psalms. Watch your step, was the message. Scotland's old ally France may still be Catholic but Scotland is now Protestant. So be careful, popish queen! It was a bad omen. There was bound to be trouble for the young queen. The leader of the singers was a short man with a long beard. His name was John Knox.

The Reformation had come late to Scotland. It started when a young man called Patrick Hamilton brought Protestant ideas back with him from Europe, where he had been a student. You can still see the place in St Andrews where the Catholic Church burned him to death for his beliefs in 1528. It took him six hours to die in a botched execution. But it was St Andrews' next martyr, George Wishart, whose death lit the fire that would finally consume the Catholic Church in Scotland. Wishart was a kind man who had given the sheets off his bed to the poor of Cambridge when he was a student there. His goodness did not prevent the Church from arresting him for his Protestantism. And in 1546 he also was burned at the stake. Cardinal Beaton, head of the Church in Scotland, watched the execution from his window in St Andrews Castle. Maybe he was checking its efficiency. This time they made sure. They filled Wishart's pockets with gunpowder to make him burn more quickly.

A few months after Wishart's death a band of Protestants stormed the castle and stabbed Cardinal Beaton to death in revenge. Others joined them and barricaded themselves in. One of them was John Knox, the man we met outside Queen Mary's window in Edinburgh. He was a former Catholic priest who had been strongly influenced by the Protestantism of George Wishart.

Knox had come late to the Bible. Two books shouted at him like the headlines in today's paper, Daniel in the Old Testament and Revelation, the last book in the New Testament. Daniel had been written during the persecution of Israel by King Antiochus in around 167 BCE, Revelation during the persecution of the young Christian Church by the Emperor Domitian at the end of the first century CE. Both books were written in a code only the persecuted could understand, strengthening them to hold fast against their enemies. Things are bad, but it's the darkness before the dawn, the last battle in a war they will win. God is coming to rid the earth of the beast that had tried to devour his children. Knox was electrified. These books weren't about the past. They were about what was happening in Scotland now! The Catholic Church was King Antiochus! It was the Emperor Domitian! The task was not to reform the Catholic Church but to destroy it and replace it with something utterly different.

In a sermon he preached in St Andrews he quoted the coded language of Daniel:

> The ten horns out of this kingdom are ten kings that shall arise: and another shall rise after them ... And he shall speak great words against the most High, and shall wear out the saints of the most High ... and they shall be given into his hand until a time and times and the dividing of time.

Wasn't that happening to them even as he spoke?

He then turned to the Beast in Revelation:

> I saw the beast, and the kings of the earth, and their armies ... And the beast was taken, and with him the false prophet that wrought miracles before him ... These both were cast alive into a lake of fire burning with brimstone. ...

For Knox, this wasn't about the dead past in Israel. It was about today in St Andrews. Judgment was coming upon Scotland. People had to take sides. There could be no compromise. You were either for God or for the Catholic Beast that stood against him. There was no middle way, 'na middis', as Knox expressed it in the Scots tongue. It's the first time we hear Knox's voice. But it might have been the last.

In 1547 when all this was happening Scotland was still a Catholic country. It was governed by the Queen Regent, Mary of Guise, mother of Mary Queen of Scots. She saw the Protestant reformers as a threat to her daughter's accession to the throne. So she sought the aid of the French in her moment of need. They arrived by ship and ended the siege in St Andrews. Knox was arrested and sentenced to two years on the French galleys. Galleys were about 150 feet long and 30 feet wide. They were equipped with sails, but when the wind failed they relied on the rowers, six men on each side fettered to an oar where they ate, slept and relieved themselves. After nearly two years on the galleys Knox was released. But he decided not to return to Scotland, now reinforced by the French. He spent the next few years working for the Protestant cause in England. And when things got hot during Bloody Mary's reign he escaped to Geneva where Protestants were in control.

He came back to Scotland in May 1559 when the Protestant cause was close to success. Again it was a sermon by Knox that set the tone for the final phase of the struggle. The Queen Regent was still battling to keep Scotland Catholic for her daughter Mary. When she tried to ban Protestant preachers, Knox came to Perth to preach. For Knox, the images and statues in Catholic churches were not innocent art. They were blasphemy, insults to God, further evidence that Catholicism had given itself to the Beast. Knox was as obsessed with idols as the Prophet Muhammad and for the same reason. They provoked the jealousy of the one true God who had denounced them in the Second Commandment.

His sermon started a riot. They stripped the church of its imagery, tore down its altars and smashed its statues. It was the beginning of an orgy of destruction that left Scotland with hardly any of the art created during its long Catholic history. The Protestant Kirk would worship in simple whitewashed buildings with no images to distract it from listening to God's word from the Bible, the only source of stimulation it trusted.

The struggle between Catholics and Protestants seemed set to continue in Scotland. Then suddenly it was over. The Queen Regent died and the Scottish nobles made a deal. Scotland would become a Protestant country in the severe form Knox wanted. But it would allow the Queen Regent's daughter Mary to return as queen and keep her Catholic faith. She could hear Mass in private, but in public she must govern Scotland as a Protestant nation. It was a political compromise. And as we've seen, Knox didn't like compromise. Now Minister of St Giles, half a mile up the hill from Holyrood Palace, Knox wasn't happy when Catholic Mary came back as Scotland's Queen. That's why he was outside her window the night she returned, singing psalms against her.

But it was over for both of them. Knox continued to preach against the compromise the Scottish nobles had made with Mary Queen of Scots. He was afraid she would find a way to smuggle the Papal Beast into the pure temple of Scottish Protestantism. She was a young woman consoled by the practice of her Catholic faith and baffled by the hatred it provoked in this man who ranted against her so frequently. The encounters between John Knox and Mary Queen of Scots show how religion can provoke conflict between otherwise good and sympathetic people. Knox was far from being a bad man. He too had suffered for his religion. But he saw everything in black and white. No grey. No middle way. Na middis!

And the accident of royal blood had sent Mary, buffeted by loss and longing for love, into a confrontation with a religion that scorched her but never won her heart. In her need to be cherished, she made bad choices. In 1565 when she was twenty-two she married her Catholic cousin Lord Darnley, a bad-tempered, unpopular drunkard. Knox preached against the marriage. In 1566 she gave birth to Darnley's son James who, as James VI of Scotland and James I of England, would one day unite the two monarchies. Darnley was murdered in 1567. Mary's next husband, Lord Bothwell, was another rogue who first abducted and then deserted her. The sequence of marital disasters was too much for the

Scottish nobles. The Queen was threatening the stability of the nation. She was arrested and forced to abdicate in favour of her son James.

And the curtain went up on the last act of her tragedy. She escaped and headed for England, confident that her cousin Queen Elizabeth would help. But she'd misjudged that as well. To Elizabeth, Mary's presence was a threat. Elizabeth had achieved a level of religious stability in England. She had managed the political fall-out of the Reformation with great care. She didn't persecute Catholics the way her sister Bloody Mary had persecuted Protestants. But the balance was precarious. And Mary Queen of Scots might threaten it. She could become a focus of Catholic ambition and discontent. Why not establish Mary on the throne of an England returned to Catholicism? She was a real queen. Elizabeth was the daughter of Anne Boleyn, and there were many who did not believe Henry's marriage to Anne had been valid. A case could be made against Elizabeth and for Mary as the rightful Queen of England.

So Elizabeth kept Mary under guard in a series of country houses in England for the next nineteen years. But when she heard Mary might be conspiring to replace her on the throne she acted. Mary was beheaded in 1587. For her execution, she insisted on wearing red, the colour of Catholic martyrs. It took several blows to remove her head from her body. And when the executioner lifted up her head in the customary gesture to prove her death he was left clutching a wig, with Mary's head still in the basket.

Europe's religious wars rumbled on for centuries, Catholics against Protestants, Protestants against other Protestants. But now and then through the fog of war there emerged a group that transcended the hatred and political conflict the Reformation had generated. One of them acquired a nickname that became famous, Quakers. We'll look at them next and it will take us across the Atlantic to America.

CHAPTER 32

Friends

It's wrong to assume that when the voice of God speaks in a human mind the result has to be on the scale of a Hollywood epic like the Exodus of the Israelites from Egypt or the Prophet Muhammad's flight from Mecca or Martin Luther's attack on indulgences in Wittenberg. Sometimes the voice commands something so personal it's a surprise anyone remembers it. Yet it can change history.

That's how it was for George Fox, one of the most attractive figures in the history of religion. It was a time in seventeenth-century England when the mighty in Church and society gave themselves airs and graces. They loved titles and the vestments that came with them. They insisted on inferiors bending their knees and sweeping off their hats in deference to them. The titles they gave themselves emphasised how far above the common herd they were. Your Holiness, Your Excellency, Your Grace, Your Majesty were forms of address that set them above the ordinary humans who scurried like ants beneath their feet. Among Christians this attitude was both surprising and unsurprising. It was surprising because it went against the clear teaching of Jesus who had told them that self-importance had no place among his disciples. But it was unsurprising because it was the world's way and religion usually goes the world's way no matter how many sacred robes it hides in.

At first the Reformation that hit Europe in the fifteenth and sixteenth centuries looked as if it might challenge all this self-importance. And to some extent it did. But the churches that rejected the authoritarianism of Rome soon found other ways of asserting their superiority. There were sects that earned the nickname *Puritan* for that very reason. They believed that they alone were the true Christians, the pure ones. Of all the forms of superiority crafted by human vanity religious superiority is the most insufferable.

Claims to spiritual or social superiority failed to impress George Fox. The voice of God told him not to take off his hat to anyone high or low or to use special forms of address to them. He was to say 'thee' or 'thou' to everyone, whether rich or poor, great or small. And because he would not bow or scrape to them he was repeatedly imprisoned by those infuriated by his refusal to acknowledge their superiority. On one occasion when he was brought to court for his insolence he announced that the only authority he trembled before was God. So the judge sarcastically dismissed him as a *quaker*. Fox's followers called themselves the Society of Friends, but the judge's insult stuck and they became known as Quakers, a title they use to this day.

George Fox had been born in Leicestershire in England in 1624. His father was a weaver and he himself had been apprenticed as a shoemaker. Like many prophets before him, when he was a young man he left home to seek enlightenment. It was a time of religious turmoil. The spiritual marketplace was noisy with the cries of religious vendors shouting the uniqueness of their own brand of faith. And though they all opposed each other, they had one thing in common. Each claimed that their version of Christianity was the one that guaranteed access to God. The implication being that to find God you needed a go-between, a friend at court to introduce you.

When he was twenty-four, Fox received a revelation that showed him he had been wasting his time searching for someone to get him through the door into God's presence. He had been looking outside himself when the answer had been closer to him than his own breathing. He didn't need to go through any of the operators who had set themselves up as God's official doorkeepers. He needed neither old priest nor new preacher to bring him into the presence of God. The door was already open. All he had to do was walk through it.

There was no need for a church, or 'steeplehouse' as Fox described it. And the paraphernalia of religion was a distraction, whether the black gowns of ministers or the coloured vestments of priests, the elaborate ceremonies of Catholicism or the dour simplicities of Protestantism. Nor did men and women need creeds or lists of things to believe. And they certainly didn't need a religious police force to enforce them! All they had to do was sit in silence with each other and wait for the Holy Spirit to speak in their hearts. God's light already burned within each of them.

All that was revolutionary enough. Were it to catch on it would wipe out organised religion. But there was more. There was the outrageous claim that all human beings were of equal worth, male and female, *slave or free!* Neither Church nor State was ready to accept George Fox's revelations, but his Quaker friends started living them in their own lives. And it cost them dear. Thousands of them were imprisoned for their beliefs and many of them died in jail. Undeterred, they fought to improve the lives of the poor. In a harsh age, they campaigned for better treatment for prisoners and the mentally ill. But it was their opposition to slavery that had the most profound impact on history. And it began in America.

By the early seventeenth century, North America had become a haven for religious groups fleeing persecution in Europe and searching for another Promised Land. The great European invasion of the New World had begun and English Quakers were among the earliest arrivals. Notable among them was William Penn, who in 1682 established a colony in what became known as Pennsylvania.

But European settlers brought more than Christianity to North America. They also brought with them one of the greatest of human evils, slavery. It was an ancient and universal cruelty, but European colonisation of the Americas gave it a new impetus. To cultivate the unforgiving land they had acquired the colonists needed labourers whom they could drive like beasts until they dropped. Slaves were the solution and there were plenty of them available.

The ships that plied the so-called Middle Passage brought millions of them from the West coast of Africa to work the sugar fields of the West Indies and the plantations in the southern states of America. Manacled together and penned in airless holds, thousands of African captives died during their passage across the Atlantic. If the weather was dangerous enough the captain might lighten his load by throwing manacled slaves overboard. Better drown slaves than let the safety of the ship be threatened. That was a last resort, of course. Slaves were a valuable commodity. Get them to the Caribbean or the Carolinas and they could be traded for other commodities such as sugar and cotton. By the eighteenth century Britain dominated the trade. It made colossal fortunes for the Christian slave masters of Scotland and England. And when they finally came home to live in forgetful retirement they built grand palaces in which to spend their declining years, many of them still gracing the British countryside. How did these Christians justify being part of such an evil business?

As we have already seen, slavery was taken for granted in the Bible. It was the way things were. It was not consistent with the message of Jesus, but the first Christians had a valid excuse for doing nothing about it. They didn't expect the world and the way it organised itself to be around for much longer. Jesus would soon be back to inaugurate God's kingdom when things would be done on earth as they were in heaven. Meanwhile, Christians should lead pure lives and hold themselves ready for the End. And leave the world as it was. We've already noted that Paul sent the slave Onesimus back to his owner Philemon. Be kind to him, he pleaded. He is now a fellow believer in Jesus. But there was never any suggestion he should set him free. What would be the point when all things were coming to an end anyway?

By 1688 it should have occurred to Christians that Jesus hadn't returned and didn't look as if he'd be back any time soon. Surely it was time to tackle the world's evils instead of waiting for God to fix them at the End Time. Except that where slavery was concerned there was a problem. The Bible had recorded what the voice of God had said to Moses on the subject:

When you buy a Hebrew slave, six years shall he serve; and in the seventh shall he go out free, for nothing. If he came in by himself, he shall go out by himself: if he were married, then his wife shall go out with him. If his master has given him a wife, and she has borne him sons or daughters, the wife and the children shall be her master's.

And Paul, in his letter to the Church in Ephesus, had advised Christian slaves to be obedient to their earthly masters 'as if to Christ himself'.

That was clear enough. Who were they to challenge it? Well, in 1688 the Pennsylvanian Quakers did challenge it. And the way they did it had a revolutionary effect on how Christians would read the Bible in the future. Quakers believed in the authority of the inner light, or what we might call conscience. And they knew by the light that guided them that slavery was just plain wrong. If all people were of equal value then it was wrong to treat some of them as less than human, as property rather than as children of God. And if the Bible said otherwise *then the Bible was wrong*!

The Quakers did more than protest against the Bible's justification of slavery. They did everything they could to overturn slavery itself. They ended it in Pennsylvania and they helped to organise the Underground Railroad that helped runaway slaves from the south find freedom in the north or in Canada. It took the world a long time to catch up with the Quakers' outrage at the existence of slavery in a so-called Christian society. It wasn't until 1833 that it was outlawed in the British Empire. And it took another thirty years before it was prohibited in the USA after the Civil War in 1865.

But the Quakers had done more than bring about the end of slavery. They had also ended a childish way of reading the Bible. By asserting their conscience against it they made it possible to study it like any other book and not as an untouchable idol. They knew the difference between what was right and what the Bible said was right. And since they believed it was God who had alerted them to the difference, it followed that God had reservations about the Bible as well! If the Bible was wrong on slavery, might it not also be wrong about a Six Day Creation? Maybe we've been reading it in the wrong way for centuries. Maybe it needs to be interpreted and read more intelligently. And maybe we should not fear asserting our own conscience against some of its judgments.

In these ways the Quakers gave a push to what is now known as the historical-critical study of scripture. It does not necessarily rule out God's influence on the Bible, but it does try to separate the human elements from the divine. Slavery was a human invention. Loving your neighbour as yourself was a divine command. Go figure!

The Society of Friends may be one of the smallest denominations in the world but its influence is enormous. It remains Christianity's conscience. It brought a new and challenging version of Christianity to America. But America had its own spirituality before Christianity arrived. It's time to look at it.

CHAPTER 33

Made in America

Christopher Columbus 'discovered' America in 1492. That suggests no one knew it was there until he found it. Europeans certainly didn't know it was there. Columbus was trying to find a passage to India when he made his historic voyage. He knew India lay east of Europe after a long voyage round the southern tip of Africa. But he hoped that if he sailed far enough west he might come at it from another, easier direction. And when he made landfall in the New World he thought he'd hit India. So he called the inhabitants Indians, a label that stuck.

Being 'discovered' was catastrophic for Native Americans, the 'Indians' who already lived there. Over the next four hundred years white settlers took over their country and carpeted it with Christianity in its many competing forms. Religion serves many purposes, some benign, some cruel. Its cruellest is to justify supplanting other races and expelling them from their homes. Like the Israelites who conquered the Promised Land of Palestine, the pioneers who pushed themselves west across North America believed it was their God-directed destiny to do so. The Protestantism they took with them was a restless religion that imprinted its character on the USA itself. It created a culture driven by desire, forever dissatisfied and constantly on the make. There were always new frontiers to conquer.

But the land the invaders overran wasn't a religious vacuum. Its natives had their own spiritual traditions, the polar opposite of the dynamic Protestantism that attacked them. Native Americans went with the grain of nature, not against it. They had a sacred connection to the land that sustained them. They believed it was animated by the Great Spirit, their term for God. This was especially true of the horse-riding tribes who lived on a huge stretch of land in the middle of the continent known as the Great Plains. Three thousand miles long and up to seven hundred miles wide, it covered an area of well over a million square miles, stretching from Canada in the north to Mexico in the south. And it was roamed by herds of buffalo that supplied almost all the needs of the people who shared the vast space with them. They were nomads who saw their relationship with the buffalo as a kind of communion. They lived lightly on the face of the earth. And while they had little desire to define or control the Great Spirit, they liked to open themselves to its mystery and experience the ecstasy it provoked. They had prophets who went off on vision quests and used drugs and rituals of self-wounding to expose themselves to its power. And they would come back to their people and repeat in dance and chant what they had encountered in their communing with the Great Spirit.

But it is wrong to see this as a 'religion', as something held separately from the rest of their lives in a compartment labelled 'faith'. They did not possess a religion in that sense. They felt themselves to be enclosed in a living mystery that included the earth and the buffalo and the wind that stirred the grasses of the high plains. And it was as fragile as it was elusive. It would not survive the invasion of the settlers and their systematic slaughter of the buffalo, a plan intended to starve them into retreat. They were not like the Puritans, who had been persecuted for their faith in England but were able to bring it with them when they crossed the Atlantic. When the Plains Indians were driven off their land and saw the buffalo hunted to extinction they lost everything.

Their tragedy prompted an outbreak of apocalyptic fervour that is heartbreaking to remember. Apocalyptic movements always brew among oppressed people who can't believe God will continue to ignore their suffering for much longer. So they dream dreams of the restoration that's on its way. In 1889 a movement broke out among the dispossessed Indians of the Plains called Ghost Dancing. The prophet who announced it told them that if they danced long and hard enough all the white people would be buried forever beneath a deep layer of new earth. All gone! The invaders obliterated! Then herds of wild horses and buffalo would return to the plains to wander again among the whispering grasses. And all the Indians who had ever been would come back to life and live with them in Paradise.

Note what Paradise was. It wasn't a heaven above where they would enjoy unimaginable pleasures. It was the life they'd had before the white man came to destroy it. So they danced. But Paradise didn't come. They danced harder and harder. Some of them danced themselves to death. But the earth did not fall upon the white people and bury them and their cruel ways. Wild horses did not sweep over the crest of a beloved hill, their manes flashing in the sun. Buffalo did not thunder out of the north calling them to the thrill and communion of the chase. The irony is that, as a result of recent conservation policies, the buffalo are now back on the Great Plains. The Indians are gone forever.

Apocalyptic movements like the Ghost Dance are cries of longing for an end to suffering. The fact that the end never comes does not kill the yearning. We find it in the religion of the USA's other crucified race, African Americans. They had been wrenched from their homes and transported thousands of miles across the ocean to serve the needs of their Christian slave masters. One of the ironies of religious history is that the Christian faith the slaves adopted from their masters was truer to the original than anything their owners could possibly understand.

Judaism had started as a slave religion. The voice that spoke to Moses from the burning bush told him to free his children from Egypt and lead them to the Promised Land. How could a slave *owner* respond sympathetically to that? But imagine you are a *slave* listening to the story for the first time. You are hearing your own story! This is about you! You get it in a way the overseer slashing his whip over your back can never understand, no matter how many hymns he sings in his white church on Sunday. Judaism was the faith of a people who longed for liberation from bondage. So did the African American slaves. They made it their own. And they sang songs about it.

> Go down, Moses,
> Way down in Egypt land,
> Tell old Pharaoh,
> To let my people go.

Christianity also began as a liberation movement. Jesus was God's agent for bringing on earth a kingdom unlike anything yet seen in history. It would put down the mighty from their seats and exalt the humble and meek. It would replace the way of oppression with the way of justice. It would heal the sick and liberate captives. And it would be brought about by a Messiah who would be whipped and taunted as he carried his cross to Calvary.

Listening to these words, how could the slaves fail to hear them as a description of their own condition? Their masters might possess the book the words came from but it was the slaves who owned their meaning. Christianity was a religion for slaves! How could slave owners get it, let alone live it? They denied it every day of their privileged lives. Slaves lived it every day! They knew it was theirs. They might not yet be able to *read* the Bible but they knew how to *be* the Bible. Its longing for liberation was their longing.

Then something else started to happen in the way they used it. The Bible sang of their yearning to be free, certainly. It echoed their longing for something they did not yet have and might never have. But they started using it in their worship in a way that gave them freedom within the system that imprisoned them. Their preachers did not just *talk about* the stories in the Bible. They made them *present*, made them real in a way that enabled their listeners to enter and feel them. In doing so they invented America's greatest art form, a way of making music about suffering that eclipsed the very suffering it sang about – if only for an hour or two on a Sunday evening in a shack on a southern plantation. They escaped from the whip and the taunt into an ecstasy that transported them to another place.

> Steal away, steal away, steal away to Jesus!
> Steal away, steal away home,
> I ain't got long to stay here.

They were enacting another of religion's purposes, its ability to console and sweeten the lot of those who bear unendurable sorrow. The nineteenth-century philosopher Karl Marx, one of its greatest critics, approved of this side of religion. He wanted to rid the world of the injustices that caused the pain religion soothed. He described religion as 'the opium of the people'. He saw it as an anaesthetic. But there are times when we need an anaesthetic. If you ever have to undergo an operation you'll welcome the doctor who puts you to sleep before the surgeon cuts you open. Religion can be a drug that soothes the pain of existence. Only an ungenerous mind would fail to sympathise with those whose misery is eased in this way. Only a heart of stone would be unmoved by the sight of a congregation of slaves finding consolation in the promise of Jesus to take them home.

But that wasn't the only use African Americans made of Judeo-Christianity and its stories. They did something more directly political with it. They used its message to campaign against the racism and injustice of twentieth-century America. For them America was still Egypt land and they were still in bondage. Their new Moses was the preacher Martin Luther King who called on old Pharaoh yet again to let his people go.

King was born in 1929 in Atlanta, Georgia, the heartland of the segregated southern states of the USA. In 1954 he became minister of a Baptist church in Montgomery, Alabama, and it was here he started the movement to fight for full civil rights for African Americans. On the eve of his assassination in 1968 Martin Luther King likened himself to the Moses who had seen the Promised Land from afar but who had died before he could enter it. For King, African Americans had made their escape from Egypt when slavery was abolished in 1865 but a hundred years on they were still far from the Promised Land of full equality. And more than half a century on from his death they still haven't made it.

As we have seen so often in this book, religion may begin with mystical experiences but it always leads to politics. It starts with the voice heard by the prophets who are its chosen instruments. And what they hear always leads to actions that affect the way people live: with politics. Sometimes the politics are bad. People are persecuted for following the wrong faith or for listening to the wrong voice. Or they are forced to embrace the message announced by the latest hot prophet. So the history of religion becomes a study in different forms of oppression.

But sometimes the politics are good. They are about liberation, not oppression. We saw good politics in the stand the Pennsylvanian Quakers made against slavery in 1688. And in the African American Church today the politics of Christianity are still about liberation. The tactics of Moses and the promises of Jesus are used to make the world a better place. Religion is no longer used as an opiate to dull the pain of injustice and inequality but as a stimulant to overcome it. That's what keeps many people in the religion game.

And it's a game Americans love to play. In the nineteenth and twentieth centuries new religions emerged in the USA. We'll look at some of them in the next few chapters.

CHAPTER 34

Born in the USA

I live in Edinburgh and I like to walk. I prefer to head for the hills that lie outside the city, but if I haven't got time for that I walk the streets near my home. Several times a month I am solicited by young men. They always operate in pairs. They always wear smart business suits, shirts and ties. They are always polite. Their accents are always American. And they always ask the same questions: Would I like to find out about Jesus Christ? Would I like to know more about the Bible? I usually refuse gently and move on. But I know I'll be accosted again and again on my walks round the neighbourhood. I don't get angry. I know they have come to Scotland as missionaries. I know they want to save me.

They know nothing about me, but I know a fair bit about them. I know they are Mormons from the Church of Jesus Christ of the Latter-Day Saints. I know their base is in Salt Lake City in Utah, a western state in the USA. And I know that every male member of the Church has to spend two years doing missionary work at home or abroad. That's why I am polite to the young men who try to convert me. They are far from home, working in a cold climate, in a country they know little about, trying to persuade me that Jesus is coming back. I've heard that before, of course, but not in the way they tell it. They inform me that when Jesus returns he'll head not for Jerusalem but for America. And it won't be his first visit. He's been there before.

How do they know that? Where did they pick up this information? They got it the way all religious ideas enter the world. From a prophet who saw visions and heard voices and wrote down what had been revealed to him. And persuaded others to believe it. He was an American. His name was Joseph Smith. He was born in 1805 in Sharon, Vermont, to a family of small-time farmers who later moved to upstate New York. As a boy he was troubled by the divisions and rivalries among the Protestant churches in his town. How was he to choose between them?

Like the prophets who came before him he went apart to pray about his problem and as he prayed he had a vision. An angel told him to keep clear of the local churches. They had departed from the vision of Jesus. Corrupt ideas had entered Christianity after the death of the first apostles and it had lost its way. But restoration was coming and he would be its instrument. He should hold himself in readiness. When the time was ripe he would restore the Church to its original purity and set it again on the true path.

So he waited. And when he was twenty-five the clinching revelation came. An angel told him of the existence of a collection of writings from the prophets of ancient America. Sometime in the fourth century a book had been inscribed onto golden plates and buried in a hill in Palmyra, New York, by a man called Mormon. It contained material going back centuries before Christ. It told the story of the Nephites and other tribes from the Middle East who had escaped to America in the ancient past. The angel who imparted this knowledge to Joseph Smith was called Moroni. As Smith later discovered, Moroni featured in the book whose existence he had revealed to him. After dying in battle Moroni had been resurrected and promoted to angelic status. And it was in his angelic role that he had alerted Smith to the existence of the golden plates of the Book of Mormon.

It is claimed that Smith unearthed the plates four years later and set about translating them into English. After three months he had produced over five hundred pages of what became known as the Book of Mormon. His version of a book said to have been compiled between 311 and 385 reads like another famous translation from twelve hundred years later, the King James Bible of 1611, loved by Protestant churches and one Smith would have been familiar with. These verses from the Book of Mormon give the tone:

> For it shall come to pass, saith thy Father, that at that day whosoever will not repent and come unto my Beloved Son, them will I cut off from among my people, O house of Israel. And I will execute vengeance and fury upon them, even as upon the heathen, such as they have not heard.

The Book of Mormon belongs among other apocalyptic texts announcing the return of Jesus Christ and the gathering of everything under his rule – the difference being that this time the new Zion would be established in America. No surprise there, once we learn from the Book of Mormon that God had shifted his plan from the Middle East to the American West. And it was to confirm America's status as the new Holy Land that Jesus had himself paid a personal visit to the continent in 34, a few months after his resurrection. The Book tells us that 'Jesus Christ did show himself unto the people of Nephi, as the multitude were gathered together in the land Bountiful, and did minister unto them . . .' This was strong stuff. The world had to be given the news. So Joseph Smith launched his gospel in Fayette, New York, on 6 April 1830. He saw his movement not as a new church but as a purification of the old. The first Christians had called themselves saints. His members were also saints, the saints of today. So the Church of Jesus Christ of the Latter-Day Saints was born. And the Book of Mormon was its bible.

As we've seen throughout this book, launching a new religious movement is bad for your health. People don't like to be told their religion is wrong. Jesus himself had said that prophets were not without honour except among their own people. It's hard to believe that someone you've known all your life has been called by God to be a prophet. And Smith was no exception to the rule. Who did he think he was? The leaders of the other churches were outraged by his claims. He and his followers were thrown in jail and hunted from town to town. But the revelations kept coming. More books were added to the shelf of Mormon scriptures. It was sex that finished him in the eyes of other Christians. It is one thing to say an angel has revealed a new bible to you. It's another thing when it tells you to take other men's wives.

Smith was told by his angel that the Church of the Latter Day Saints was the restoration of the true faith of ancient Israel. Since Abraham and the other patriarchs had had many wives he must follow their example and restore the biblical practice of polygamy that permitted a man to have several wives at the same time. Smith obeyed and acquired up to forty wives, some of them already married to other men in the Church.

It was the last straw to his opponents. To escape persecution in the east, Smith moved his flock west into Illinois and Ohio, where in 1836 the first Mormon temple was built. He found it hard to keep ahead of those who were after him and had to keep moving. Finally in 1844, in Carthage, Illinois, during one of his frequent spells in prison he and his brother Hyrum were murdered. But it was far from the end of the Church he had started. The blood of the martyrs is always the seed of the Church. In 1847 the Mormons chose Brigham Young to be their new leader. If Smith was the prophet of Mormonism, Young was its consolidator, the man who built the systems that gave it enduring life.

Young was born in Vermont in 1801, the ninth of eleven children. He was one of those brilliantly practical men who could turn their hand to anything. And when he was baptised into the Church of Jesus Christ of the Latter Day Saints in 1832 he put his formidable talents at the disposal of the new movement. In his work of restoration of the Church, Smith had established a governing group of twelve apostles. Young was ordained an apostle in 1835. Recognising his abilities, Smith put him in charge of the business operations of the Church. One of the intriguing things about Mormonism is that from the beginning it had a hard-headed business approach to managing its affairs in the world.

The challenge that faced Young when he took over after Smith's assassination was how to secure the safety of the Church. His solution was to take it even further west to Utah, then under the control of Mexico. Utah might be the Mormons' Promised Land, but it was already occupied by Ute Indians. To begin with that didn't bother Smith. The Book of Mormon had informed him that Indians were the descendants of the Israelites who had come to America hundreds of years before Christ. So the Utes were the successors of the people Jesus Christ had addressed when he called on them after his resurrection. This meant that, unlike the other settlers who invaded the American West, Mormons were not hostile to the Indians they encountered. They were already a part of their religious story. They planned to convert them and complete the mission Jesus had started eighteen hundred years before.

So Brigham Young led his exodus of wagon trains of thousands of Mormons into their new Zion, eager to meet those ancient Israelites. It was soon obvious that what the Mormons wanted from the Utes and what the Utes wanted for themselves were not compatible. It became another of those encounters that proved to be catastrophic for Native Americans all over the continent. Young recognised that what he called the 'habits of civilisation' were not compatible with the Utes' way of life. And it was the habits of civilisation that had to prevail. The Utes were herded into reservations and Utah became the Mormon Holy Land.

When Utah was taken over by the United States at the end of its war with Mexico, Young became its first governor. The Church of the Latter Day Saints had finally secured its homeland. But there was a price to pay. Like Smith before him, Young was a polygamist. He'd had twenty wives and had fathered forty-seven children. If he wanted the Mormons of Utah to be left in peace to practise their faith they would have to compromise with a federal government that would have no truck with polygamy. They renounced it, though its lure never completely faded. In the history of Mormonism there have always been some who have tried to restore it to the life of the Church as part of Joseph Smith's original vision. They've usually failed, but there was a consolation prize. Polygamy is still practised in heaven. If a man's wife dies on earth and he marries again, he gets to keep both of them in the afterlife.

The Church of the Latter Day Saints had a colourful start but they're a sober outfit today. Mormons don't smoke tobacco or use any other kind of drug. They don't drink alcohol, tea or coffee. They're not allowed tattoos or piercings. They don't gamble. They don't have sex before marriage. They value family life and have lots of children when they marry. They work hard and many of them have become very wealthy. And their young men give two years of their lives to missionary work at home in the USA or abroad in other countries. You might even bump into some of them in a street near you.

CHAPTER 35

The Great Disappointment

Joseph Smith was not the only prophet in the state of New York in the nineteenth century. And the Church of the Latter Day Saints was not the only new religion to come into existence there. There was a lot of excitement around but its enthusiasts didn't always look in the same direction. Smith had dug up a new version of the past. But there were those who looked forward, not back. They weren't interested in the past. It was the future they concentrated on. Because all those promises in the Bible about the return of Christ were about to be fulfilled! He was coming back! And soon!

The man who was most certain of this was William Miller of Low Hampton. Miller was a compulsive reader of the Bible. He was fascinated by the strand in both Old and New Testaments that predicted the return of the Christ to judge the living and the dead. He became persuaded that the Bible contained a hidden code that would give him the precise date of the Second Coming if only he could interpret it correctly. We've already seen that Daniel is the book to read if you want to play this game. And that's just where Miller found the clue he was looking for.

In the eighth chapter of Daniel the prophet had written: 'Unto two thousand and three hundred days; then shall the sanctuary be cleansed'. Miller was sure that was the code he was looking for. It meant 2,300 years! Counting forward he arrived at 21 March 1844 for Christ's return. He got ready for it. But it didn't happen. He decided his calculation must have been slightly out, so he made it again. This time he came up with 22 October the same year. That day came and went. Again nothing happened. To Miller and his followers his failure became known as the Great Disappointment. Sensibly, Miller retired from the prediction game.

Others kept it going and in 1860 they formed themselves into a new denomination with its own prophet. They called themselves Seventh Day Adventists. Adventists, because they continued to believe that Jesus would be back soon, though they couldn't be sure of the date. And Seventh Day because they kept Saturday, not Sunday, as their Sabbath. They blamed the Catholic Church for changing the Sabbath from the last to the first day of the week. But switching Sabbaths was the least of their charges against the Church of Rome. They agreed with the Scottish reformer John Knox that Rome was the Anti-Christ.

The prophet of the Adventists was Ellen White. Born in 1827, she died in 1915 and the writings she left have biblical authority among Seventh Day Adventists. Like many sects, they followed a strict moral code that included vegetarianism as well as prohibitions against smoking, drinking, dancing and most forms of entertainment. They believed in the Trinity and in the divinity of Christ. And they looked for Christ's coming again in power and great glory. But they were unorthodox in their beliefs about what happened after death.

Official Christian doctrine was that on the Day of Judgment humans would be separated into two groups. One group would spend eternity in Hell because of their wickedness, while the righteous would enjoy eternal bliss in Heaven. Ellen White rejected that doctrine. She wrote:

How repugnant to every emotion of love and mercy, and even to our sense of justice, is the doctrine that the wicked dead are tormented with fire and brimstone in an eternally burning hell; that for the sins of a brief earthly life they are to suffer torture as long as God shall live.

Rather than sending sinners to eternal torment, White said, God consigned them to eternal oblivion. Annihilation and not ever-lasting agony was the fate of the sinner: 'There will then be no lost souls to blaspheme God as they writhe in never-ending torment; no wretched beings in hell will mingle their shrieks with the songs of the saved'. Saint Thomas Aquinas would not have approved.

White's abolition of Hell was picked up by another nineteenth-century American who was looking for the end of the world. Charles Taze Russell was a Pittsburgh shopkeeper who had been influenced by William Miller's predictions. Unlike Miller he didn't admit defeat or disappointment when the Second Coming didn't happen. He solved the difficulty by saying that Christ had indeed come back but he had hidden his presence behind a cloak of invis-ibility. So these *were* the Last Days and the End Time had already begun. It would climax visibly in 1914 during the last battle at Armageddon.

Like the Scottish Reformer John Knox, Russell conflated the Old Testament prophet Daniel with the New Testament prophet John, author of the Book of Revelation. John had been exiled to the isle of Patmos during the persecution of the Church by the Roman Emperor Domitian. This is how his book opens. 'The Revelation of Jesus Christ, which God gave unto him, to show unto his servants things which must shortly come to pass . . .' John then tells us he was in a trance on the Lord's Day and heard a voice saying, 'Behold, I come as a thief. Blessed is he that watcheth . . .' The voice announced that the last battle would be fought at a 'place called in the Hebrew tongue Armageddon'. Armageddon was a field north of Jerusalem that had been the scene of several battles in Israel's history.

That was all Russell needed. In 1879 he started a movement called the Watchtower for those on the lookout for the Second

Coming and the Armageddon that would follow. They were to warn as many people as they could about what was coming, though only 144,000 would be saved. All the others, as Ellen White had prophesied, were destined for annihilation. Russell took a lot from the Adventists, but he was selective in his choices. He was glad to be rid of Hell, but he wanted rid of more than that. The Trinity had to go. God, or Jehovah as he preferred to call him, was all he needed.

Armageddon of a sort did hit Europe in 1914 at the start of the First World War. But it wasn't the one Russell expected. And when he died in 1916 he was still waiting for the real thing. The man who followed him as leader of the Watchtower was a tough businessman called Joseph R. Rutherford. He soon got Russell's followers organised for a long campaign. In 1931 he changed their name to Jehovah's Witnesses. He imposed a strict discipline that kept them separate from the society around them. He turned them away from the world and in on themselves.

It takes courage to turn your back on modern society and reject all its values, including the way it practises medicine. Jehovah's Witnesses won't accept blood transfusions. Blood is life to them and only God can give it. So they are sometimes prosecuted for refusing transfusions for their children. To stand against the world in this way can give a group a strong sense of identity. Persecution can reinforce commitment. It also makes it hard to break away from the group if you change your mind about its beliefs.

Rutherford died in 1942. Armageddon still hadn't hit, though the Second World War that was raging at the time was a good imitation. Once again the Jehovah's Witnesses weathered the disappointment. New leaders counselled them to dig in for the long haul of history. Christ will return. So keep watching. Like the Mormons, Witnesses are enthusiastic about door-to-door missionary activity. And they continue to make converts to their cause. Their places of worship are not called churches but Kingdom Halls. All over the world they continue to sell their magazine, *The Watchtower*. They remain on guard, scanning the horizon for the One who will come like a thief in the night.

Sects like the Seventh Day Adventists and the Jehovah's Witnesses remind us of one of the Bible's most awkward embarrassments: the fact that, after two thousand years of waiting and watching, Christ still hasn't come back. Liberal Christians handle the problem with some delicacy. They don't disbelieve the Second Coming. How could they? It sits solidly in their Bible. It is rehearsed in their creeds. And the month before Christmas – Advent – is given over to meditating on its meaning.

They deal with it by suggesting that God's coming kingdom is already here. What Christians have to do is look for proof of its presence. It is found where the poor are helped and injustices are challenged. It is found where good people work to make the world a better place, a place more like the kingdom described by Jesus. And there are words of Jesus that support this approach. They come from a book that didn't make it into the New Testament, though it contains genuine sayings of Jesus. It is called the Gospel of Thomas. In it the disciples ask Jesus: 'When will the kingdom come?' Jesus replies, 'It will not come by waiting for it. It will not be a matter of saying, here it is or there it is. Rather, the kingdom of the father is spread out upon the earth, and men do not see it.'

Real believers in the Second Coming find that approach feeble. They want something more full-blooded. They want Armageddon. And American Christianity has been good at supplying it. Maybe it's because Americans see themselves as a chosen nation, an exceptional people with a God-directed destiny. However we account for it, the history of Christianity in America has been full of sects looking for the end of the world and the return of Christ. And they are still at it. New prophets appear frequently, proclaiming that the end is nigh. And they find new and different ways of getting their message across. One of the most successful of them has used fiction to get the word out, in a series of novels people can pick up in their local supermarket.

The American Evangelical minister Tim LaHaye has been described as the most influential American Christian of the last forty years. What he has done is to give the Second Coming a new charge of electricity. There are sixteen novels in his 'Left Behind' series. They get their punch from their contemporary setting. They are not set in ancient Israel. They are happening right now in today's troubled and violent world. In the books, what is known as the Rapture has already happened. The End has begun. And true believers have been caught up to heaven from whatever they were doing on earth at the moment it started. If they were driving cars or piloting airplanes they were snatched from their seats and instantly transported to eternal life, leaving their vehicles below to crash in blockbusting spectaculars. The 'Left Behind' world is plunged into chaos and people start clamouring for a leader to rescue them from its horrors. And one appears. They make him Secretary-General of the United Nations because he looks like the man to bring order to the planet. What the world does not know is that he is the Anti-Christ foretold in the Bible, the great deceiver intent on leading the world astray – the Beast! In the time of the Reformation they would have made him pope. But the hate object of Evangelical Americans today is no longer the Pope. It's the United Nations. In the novels, an airline pilot and his friends soon realise what's happening. They start a fightback against the new Anti-Christ to save the lost and get them ready for the Great Tribulation that's the prelude to the Last Days. The novels have sold more than sixty-five million copies. In America there is still a lot of mileage in end-time religion.

But it's not the only kind of religion that's been going on there in the last hundred years.

CHAPTER 36

Mystics and Movie Stars

Students of religion make a distinction between a church and a sect. A church is more complicated than a sect. It has a broad range of beliefs and it tries to keep them in some sort of balance. A sect fastens on one aspect of religion and makes it their main concern. In the last chapter we saw how Seventh Day Adventists and Jehovah's Witnesses concentrated on the bits of the Bible that predicted the return of Christ to judge the world and bring on the end time. That's why classifiers pin them to the board as sects rather than churches. The Church of Christ Scientist, which was founded in Boston in the USA in 1879, is also described as a sect. It took one aspect of the work of Jesus Christ and pursued it as its main theme.

It was Jesus's work as a healer that Christian Science took as its mission. The prophet who founded the movement was born Mary Baker in 1821 in New Hampshire. Mary was a sickly child and constant illness followed her into adulthood. Like the woman in Mark's Gospel who had suffered much at the hands of physicians, Mary spent a lot of time in search of healing. As well as conventional medicine, she tried hypnotism and other alternatives. Nothing worked for long. Then in 1866 she slipped on an icy street and damaged her spine. This time she tried something different. She took her injury not to a doctor but to the New Testament. While meditating on a passage in Matthew's Gospel where Jesus commanded a paralysed man to get up and walk she herself experienced healing. Not only had her damaged spine been mended, she believed she had discovered the science that lay behind the healing work of Jesus.

The revelation that came to her was that sickness was based on an illusion. The illusion was that matter had an independent existence. It didn't. It had been created by the mind of God. Mind was the cause. Matter was the effect. So the way to find healing was by mind over matter. This is how she put it in her book, *Science and Health*: 'Human knowledge calls them forces of matter; but divine Science declares that they belong wholly to divine Mind . . . and are inherent in this Mind'. To apply the principle of mind over matter to human suffering was to recognise that the ills that afflicted us had no reality. They were deceptions, illusions, games played by matter over mind. The way to healing was not through doctors who played the same game, the material game. It came by opening ourselves to God's loving power, which would banish the illusion of illness and restore us to health and reality. Christian Science did not *heal* our illnesses. It cured us of the illusion that we ever had them in the first place!

It wasn't a doctrine that the mainstream churches in New England were prepared to accept. They didn't believe suffering could be so easily wished away. It was real, not an illusion. They suspected that Mary Baker did not believe in the reality of sin and judgment, Heaven and Hell. Nor did she. No one was beyond redemption in her book. And no problem was beyond solution once the principle of mind over matter was understood. Frustrated by their opposition to her revelations, Mary – who had married her third husband Asa Gilbert Eddy in 1877 – founded the Church of Christ, Scientist in Boston in 1879. In 1908 she founded a newspaper, the *Christian Science Monitor*, still in print and widely respected. Equally famous is the Mother Church of Christian Science which stands on a four-teen-acre site in Boston's Back Bay.

Christian Science services consist of readings from the Bible and from Mary Baker Eddy's own works, particularly *Science and Health*. There are hymns and silences, but the only form of prayer used is the Lord's Prayer. Christian Science never became a mass movement but it is widely spread throughout the world. In most cities you will find one of its reading rooms where Mary Baker Eddy's writings are on display and you can find out for yourself how to apply the principle of mind over matter to the ills that beset you. She died at her home in a Boston suburb in 1910.

Forty years later, in 1952, another American religion was born that was even more dismissive of modern medicine than Christian Science. It called itself the Church of Scientology and its prophet was a writer of science fiction called Lafayette Ronald Hubbard, who had been born in Nebraska in 1911. It is popular among Hollywood movie stars. Tom Cruise and John Travolta ascribe their success to its principles and practices. Scientology uses modern technology and mind exploration techniques, but its underlying philosophy is the ancient Hindu doctrine of reincarnation or samsāra. It believes in the existence of immortal souls called *thetans* who migrate from body to body over trillions of years. It's hard to be sure of the detail in Scientology, but thetans do not themselves appear to have been created. They themselves were the creators of the universe. And in order to operate within it they crafted vehicles for themselves, the human body being only one of the many shapes they adopted.

This is where things start to get complicated. All religions try to explain and supply a remedy for the evil and suffering in the world. The Bible blamed it on an act of disobedience, a fall from grace that ejected Adam and Eve from Eden. And human history became a search for redemption and restoration to paradise. In Hindu theology it was karma or the Law of the Deed that propelled us through millions of lives till we were purged of our sins and slipped finally into nirvāna. Scientology uses elements of both in its teaching.

In their wandering through millions of lives thetans get emotionally and psychologically battered by the experiences they undergo. It leaves them damaged, the way a brutal childhood can throw a shadow over an adult's life. Some of these damaging experiences happen by accident. Hubbard called them *engrams*. They were just the bruises time left on thetans as they travelled through their millions of lives, ordinary wear and tear. Sometimes the damage was intentional, inflicted by thetans who had gone over to the dark side and wanted power over other thetans.

Hubbard called these deliberate injuries to the human psyche *implants*. They were the main source not only of physical and psychological misery but of bad ideas deliberately planted to lead thetans astray. He wrote: 'Implants result in all varieties of illness, apathy, degradation, neurosis and insanity and are the principle causes of these in man'. He said the Christian idea of Heaven had been inserted forty-three trillion years ago. It was the result of two implants carefully engineered to deceive thetans into thinking they would get only one life rather than the infinite series that awaited them.

Engrams and implants are Scientology's version of what Christians call 'the Fall'. They account for human misery. And Scientology's cure for what afflicts us is just as specific. Engrams lock themselves into the human subconscious, or 'reactive mind' as Hubbard called it, triggering distress in our lives. Salvation comes through purging or 'clearing' them by a process called 'auditing'. That sounds like a counsellor listening to clients as they slowly uncover events in the past that cause them present distress. That's not how it works in Scientology. Auditors listen but they use technology to do so. They have a piece of kit called an *electropsychometer* or *E-meter* that works like a lie detector. The E-meter helps the auditor find the question that will bring the buried event to the surface. The goal of each session is to have a 'win' or moment of revelation. The win brings the guilty experience to the surface where it is zapped out of existence. It is not that the incident is remembered and then healed. It is removed from the memory. The past is not confessed and redeemed. It is erased.

There are other redemptive techniques in Scientology that deliver its version of salvation. But it is salvation in a specialised sense. It is limited to this life, the one the believer is going through at the moment. There is no final salvation or damnation. No Heaven. No Hell. Life is not a one-shot deal. There is only the eternal return of life after life. It is samsāra without nirvāna. What Scientology does is to help you improve the life you are on now by purging your engrams and acknowledging your implants.

But it's not cheap. You pay for these saving techniques in real cash. And they're expensive. The further and deeper into the mysteries of Scientology you go the more money you have to pay upfront. That's why critics say it's a business, not a religion. To which Scientologists reply that the other religions all have ways of getting money off people to keep them going, so why can't they? Lafayette Ron Hubbard died in 1986. Whether he came back as a Scientologist or as something else is impossible to say. So we don't know if he's still in the programme.

Religions like Scientology keep coming along, but it's hard to find much that is new in what they say. Maybe that's because, as the Old Testament book of Ecclesiastes says, there's nothing new to say about anything: 'What has been is what will be, and what has been done is what will be done; and there is nothing new under the sun'. That certainly seems to be true of the last religion I want to glance at in this chapter, the Unification Church or the Holy Spirit Association for the Unification of World Christianity, nicknamed the Moonies after its founder and prophet Sun Myung Moon. Moon was born in Korea in 1920. When he was sixteen Jesus appeared to him and told him that he had been appointed to complete his mission. Moon was very interested in sex. He believed that Eve had ruined sex for humanity by separating it from love. As well as fornicating with Adam, she'd done it with Satan. And the taint had been passed on.

So God appointed Jesus to redeem the situation. The plan was for him to marry and produce sinless children. In this way – to borrow a term from Scientology – Eve's 'implant' of sin into the human experience of sex would have been erased and Jesus and his bride would have produced sinless children. Unfortunately, Jesus was crucified before he could find the perfect mate and redeem humanity. God's plan had again been thwarted. But now it was back on track. Sun Myung Moon had been appointed as Messiah to complete the work of Jesus. And it would be done by establishing the ideal family, the purity of whose love would finally undo Eve's sin.

It took Moon until wife number four before he discovered the perfect mate and was able to begin his campaign of salvation through marriage. He then called on his disciples to follow his example. He encouraged them to do so in mass ceremonies where, for a fee, thousands of couples are wedded at a time, many of them having had their partners chosen for them. It must have been profitable. When Sun Myung Moon died in 2012 aged 92 it is said he was worth $900 million.

The Unification Church moved to the West in the 1970s and attracted many young people into its ranks. This sketch of its teaching shows how in religion the themes of Fall and Redemption are repeated and renewed. Human discontent is constantly looking for an answer to its troubles. And there's always someone waiting in the wings eager to supply it with yet another new religion. That's why it will be a relief in the next chapter to look at a movement whose intention is not to multiply religions but to bring them together.

CHAPTER 37

Opening Doors

A useful word to add to your religious vocabulary is *ecumenical*. It comes from the Greek *oikos* for a house, extended to the idea of *oikoumene* or the whole of humanity. The move is from a single family locked behind closed doors to the whole human race out there in the world. To be ecumenical is to reach out to others and celebrate what we have in common with them. It is to come out from behind closed doors and join hands with our neighbours. That kind of opening out was the big story of religion in the twentieth century. It happened in a number of places, but we'll begin with Christianity.

The Reformation of the sixteenth century had split Christians into warring groups. And when they stopped killing each other they spent the next few centuries ignoring each other. Each denomination kept to itself and got on with its own life. Then slowly the heavy doors began to open and Christians came outside and started talking to each other over their high fences. The conversation began at a conference in Edinburgh in 1910 where a number of Protestant missionary societies met to share concerns.

Then in 1938 the leaders of a hundred churches voted to form a World Council of Churches modelled on the United Nations. The outbreak of the Second World War in 1939 put that ambition on hold. But in 1948 the World Council of Churches held its first Assembly at which 147 churches were represented. Today its membership stands at 345 different denominations, a number that reminds us how fragmented Christianity still is.

In its early years the Ecumenical Movement was hoping for reunion, the bringing of divided Christian groups into a single whole, One Church. It's not a perfect analogy, but it might be thought of as an attempt to merge a number of competing firms into one big business. It was an engineering model. Take a bit off here, add a bit on there, bolt them together and behold, a United Church! A few Protestant churches did succeed in getting themselves joined up like that, such as the United Church of Christ that came together in 1957 out of two separate denominations, and the Uniting Church in Australia that came together in 1977 out of three. Apart from a few local successes, the search for this kind of unity failed. But it changed the mood between the churches.

The search for unity was succeeded by a more relaxed approach in which the churches decided that though they might not want to marry each other they saw no reason why they shouldn't become friends. It was easier if they already had things in common and were prepared to ignore the differences. In the jargon of the ecumenical movement, they then 'came into communion with each other'. So the Anglican churches of the British Isles joined in communion with the Lutheran churches of Northern Europe in 1992. They didn't merge and become a new denomination. They all stayed in their own houses. But they opened their doors to each other and became an extended family.

It's too early to say where all this ecumenical activity will take Christianity. An educated guess is that the search for an engineered unity has probably had its day. A more relaxed approach has taken over in which it is reckoned that differences between churches are something to celebrate. After all, every family has its own style and way of doing things, but they all belong to the same worldwide human community. An approach that celebrates variety is emerging. It sees little chance of welding thousands of Christian denominations into one big firm. But it is beginning to see virtue and beauty in multiplicity. Like a garden in which a hundred flowers bloom, God can be understood and worshipped in many different ways.

If this sounds more Eastern than Western, more Hindu than Christian, that's because it is. The ecumenical movement might have taken its first bow in Christianity in 1910, but the impulse behind it had been around for much longer. We have already seen it at work in Sikhism, with its open attitude towards other faith traditions. In this it reflected the Hindu metaphor of many streams making their way to the sea. That's not an idea that would have appealed to the Prophet Muhammad, who saw Islam not as one faith among others, but as their completion and fulfilment.

So it is intriguing that the most ecumenical religion on earth today had its origins not in Hinduism but in Islam. It is called Bahá'i. It dates from 1844 in Persia, or present-day Iran. Like Christianity and Islam, Bahá'i is a classical prophetic religion. The essence of prophecy is that the mind of God is revealed to specially elected men – they are usually men – who tell what they have seen and heard. And a community is formed to bring the new teaching to the world. Islam celebrates this prophetic tradition, running from Abraham through Jesus to Muhammad. But it believes Muhammad was the last prophet, the culmination or perfection of the stream of revelation, the Seal of the Prophets. The river had finally found its lake. And prophecy had ceased.

That's not how Bahá'is see it. For them there is no lake, no dam that confines God's revelation. The river is still running. Prophecy is still flowing. It will flow until the end of history. And from time to time it bubbles to the surface in revelations to a new prophet. Bahá'is believe it came to the surface in the middle of the nineteenth century in Iran when God sent his latest prophet to earth. You'll remember that the Gospels tell us that Jesus Christ had a forerunner called John the Baptist. People asked John if he was the

Messiah. He said he wasn't. But he had come to prepare the way for the one who was to come.

The same thing happened in Iran in 1844. A young man who called himself the Báb or Gate announced that he was a herald from God sent to prepare the way for the coming of the next prophet. Báb was not a prophet but he suffered the usual fate of prophets. His claim to be the Gate through which the new prophet would enter was heresy to orthodox Muslims. For them Muhammad was the last of the prophets. There could be no other. So in 1850 the Báb was arrested and executed.

A couple of years later a man called Mirza Husayn Ali Nuri, jailed for following the Báb and waiting eagerly for the prophet he had foretold, had a revelation that he himself was the prophet he was looking for. He took the name Bahá'u'lláh, meaning 'the Glory of God'. And the Bahá'i faith was born. Bahá'u'lláh fared better than the Báb. The Iranian authorities did not execute him, but he spent the next forty years forced between prison and exile. He died in the prison city of Acre in Palestine in 1892. He was another example of how starting a new religion can seriously endanger your health.

His son Abdu'l-Bahá, who had shared his imprisonment, succeeded him as leader. And when he was released from prison in 1908, he travelled widely in Egypt, Europe and America, spreading word of the new revelation and gathering followers. When he died in 1921 he was succeeded by his grandson, Shoghi Effendi. The Bahá'i faith continued to grow throughout the world. And when Shoghi Effendi died in London in 1957, the leadership of the movement passed from an individual in the prophetic succession to a group of believers known as the Universal House of Justice.

The beauty of Bahá'i is that there's nothing complicated about it. Its essential idea is that of progressive revelation. God keeps sending prophets, of whom Bahá'u'lláh just happened to be the latest. That doesn't mean Bahá'u'lláh's is the final revelation. It does mean he is the one humanity should pay attention to for the time being, because his is the latest revelation to learn from. It's a simple lesson, one that chimes with the ecumenical spirit of the time. There is one God, whose being is beyond human comprehension.

What prophets catch is a glimpse into the mind of God. Unfortunately, the religions that form themselves round these glimpses always get one thing wrong. And their mistake is always the same. They think theirs is the last word on God.

Bahá'is believe that all the world's religions have understood something of the mystery of God, so they should all be respected. Their glimpses are valid. But none gets the complete picture. Not even Bahá'i. Bahá'i just happens to be the most recent version. And it has the beauty of simplicity. It has recognised that there are many religions, but they are all looking at the same God. In that sense they are already one. And it is *what* they are looking at that unites them, not the angle from which they see it. Religions forget that. They confuse what is seen with the one who is doing the seeing. It's the parable of the blind men and the elephant all over again, thought about in a different way. The elephant may be one, but each man has a different angle on it.

So what is the Bahá'i angle? There's nothing new in saying there is one God. What Bahá'is go on to point out is that humanity is also one. The unity of the human race is as important a lesson to learn as the unity of God. And it has solid practical implications. The tragedy of religions that think they are the last word is that they divide humanity into warring blocks. Religion then becomes humanity's greatest enemy. But once it realises that although the religions all see God from different angles, it is the same God they are all seeing, religion can become a force for unity rather than division.

That's why Baháí's were prominent in the movement to bring the world's religions together in a new kind of global ecumenism called the World's Parliament of Religion. It met for the first time in Chicago in 1893 and a century later in 1993. Its most recent meeting was in Salt Lake City in October 2015. The parliament is a sign that in our era some religions are turning away from years of division and suspicion to open up a new age of friendship and conversation.

As well as their global witness to the unity of God and the unity of humanity, followers of Bahá'i have their own simple and distinctive style of spiritual practice. They don't have a dedicated priesthood. Nor do they impose doctrinal uniformity on their members. Theirs is a domestic faith, its rites followed mainly in their own living rooms. But they reflect Bahá'í's origins in Islam. After a ritual washing, Bahá'ís follow the practice of prayer facing in a particular direction. Not towards Mecca, but towards the tomb of their prophet Bahá'ulláh in Israel. And their prayer is simple. 'I bear witness, O my God, that Thou hast created me to know Thee and to worship Thee ... There is none other God but Thee, our help in peril ...'

Bahá'i illustrates a trend within religion in our time away from the divisions of the past towards a different kind of unity. Not one that comes from hammering systems together into new institutions. But by the uncovering of a unity that is already there: the unity of our common humanity. And it is discovered more by listening than by speaking. It is expressed more in silence than in noise.

But it is far from being a universal trend. It is balanced by an opposite trend. By angry fundamentalists who see themselves as the sole possessors of God's truth. And they are responsible for some of the ugliest conflicts in the world today. We'll take a look at their story in the next chapter.

CHAPTER 38

Angry Religion

Fundamentalist is a label that gets attached to several religious groups today, but it was first used in the early twentieth century to describe a particular brand of American Protestantism. Modern science was making life increasingly difficult for those Christians who took the Bible literally. The Bible had told them that God took six days to create the universe before taking the seventh day off. And that at a precise moment on the sixth day he brought forth fully formed human beings. Until the nineteenth century many thought this was the way things had actually happened. Then real scientists got into the game and began to question it. One of them gave believers a headache.

His name was Charles Darwin. In his research Darwin came to the conclusion that all the species on our planet had evolved over a very long period of time through a process of tiny adaptations to their environment. Out went a six-day creation. That was bad enough. Worse was his claim that fully formed human beings did not emerge as a special creation on one day six thousand years ago. They too had evolved slowly over millions of years. And their most recent ancestors were apes! When Darwin's book *On the Origin of Species* came out in 1859 it caused a crisis for those who read the story in the Bible not as a poem celebrating God's creation of the universe but as a precise description of how he had done it. Christians responded in different ways to Darwin's book.

Many read it and became convinced Darwin was right. So the Bible must be wrong! And the house of faith fell round their ears. Losing their religion made them sad, much the way children feel when they stop believing in Santa Claus. But other believers took a leaf out of Darwin's book and adapted their religion to the new science. They did this by learning to read the Bible in a new way. It was art not science. It was designed to make you think about life's meanings, not give you information about life's mechanics. Their religion survived, but it lost its old certainty. Which meant it became faith for the first time! Certainty is not faith. It is the opposite of faith. If you are certain of something you don't need to *believe* it. You know it. I don't *believe* 2+2=4. I *know* it. I am certain of it. I can do it on my fingers. But I can't be certain life has an overarching meaning and that the world has a creator who loves it. Or that I will go on to another life after death. None of this can be known for certain. We either believe it or we don't believe it. We have faith. Or we don't have faith. Modern science did religion a favour by helping it to understand itself better and change the way it talked about itself.

But some Christians refused to come to terms with modern science. They would neither surrender their faith to it nor find their way to a different understanding of faith because of it. They decided to fight it. Science did not make them sad. Nor did it make them think. It made them angry! And anger became the main ingredient in fundamentalism. To understand it you have to feel the fury and frustration that prompted it.

Have you ever lost your temper with a piece of malfunctioning equipment and wanted to throw it across the room? Have you ever watched a tennis player bang his racket on the court as if it were to blame for the shot he had just missed? Life constantly throws changes at us that knock us out of our comfort zone. And some people are better at handling them than others. Some adapt easily to new challenges. We call them 'early adopters'. They can't wait to get their hands on the latest phone or iPad. Others adapt more reluctantly. And some refuse to adapt at all. They hate change and fight angrily against it. Especially if it challenges cherished beliefs! Science was the greatest agent of change in the modern era, so it became the target of furious believers who felt themselves ambushed by it. Their anger boiled over in the USA between 1910 and 1925. It was Darwin's theory of evolution that started the war.

The first barrage against it was a series of pamphlets published by a group that called itself 'The World's Christian Fundamentals Association'. Fundamentals are strong foundations. If you build your house on them the floods of time will not wash it away. For the authors of the pamphlets the foundation on which Christianity was built was the infallible truth of the Bible. God had dictated every word of it and God didn't make mistakes. Everything in the Bible was true, God's own word. And any human word that contradicted it was wrong. Darwin had contradicted it. Therefore Darwin was wrong!

Fundamentalists didn't try to disprove science. They didn't *argue* against it. They *pronounced* against it! It was the equivalent of a parent clinching an argument with a child by shouting: 'because I say so'. That's what fundamentalist religion does. It refutes not by evidence but by authority. Why is Darwin wrong? Because the Bible says so! But they did more than pontificate. They tried to ban science itself. That's when science fought back.

Prompted by the angry protests of Christian Ministers, in 1925 the State of Tennessee outlawed the teaching of evolution in its schools. It became a punishable offence to teach 'any theory that denies the story of the Divine Creation of man as taught in the Bible and to teach instead that man has descended from a lower order of animals'. A young science teacher called John Thomas Scopes decided to challenge the new law. He got himself arrested for teaching his students about evolution. His plan was to use his court case to show how foolish it was to try to disprove evolution by quoting Genesis. Backed by the American Civil Liberties Union and defended by Clarence Darrow, at the time America's most famous lawyer, the Scopes case became known as the Monkey Trial because of Darwin's claim that humans were descended from apes. Scopes pleaded guilty to teaching evolution and was fined $100. Darrow used the defence to show up the contradictions in the fundamentalist position and to prove that its main spokesman didn't know what he was talking about. Scopes lost the case but Darrow won the argument. But it wasn't until 1968 that the law banning the teaching of evolution in schools was overturned by the US Supreme Court.

The Scopes trial showed how new knowledge prompted fundamentalist fury. Fundamentalists of any description don't like history and the changes it brings. They'd rather smash their rackets on the court than respond to what's coming at them from the future. The past is all they want. 'Why do you keep bringing up the future?' they cry. Fundamentalism is a tantrum. It's a screaming fit, a refusal to accept new realities.

But if scientific change and the new knowledge it brings is hard for the fundamentalist mind to accept, even harder is change in the way we run society. In our era, religious fundamentalism became more agitated by social change than by the pressures of science. And in some of its forms not only did it get angry. It got violent.

The most revolutionary change that hit the world in the twentieth and twenty-first centuries was the liberation of women. The Bible and the Qur'an came from societies controlled by men. No surprise there. That's how the world everywhere was run until fairly recently. And there is something worth noting before we go deeper into the issue. History shows that the men in charge never volunteer to give up their privileges. They don't wake up one day and say, 'I've suddenly realised that the way I control and dominate others is wrong. I must change my ways. So I'll share my power with them. I'll give them the vote!' That's never how it works. History shows that power always has to be wrested from those who have it. The suffragettes who fought for the vote or suffrage for women learned that lesson. Men didn't volunteer to give women the vote. Women had to fight them for it.

There's another thing to note about power and it's where religion comes in. The powerful love power for its own sake but they cloak their lust with theories that justify it. The theory they used to prevent women voting was that the female brain could not comprehend the complexity of politics. Politics was for men. Childbearing was for women. And the best supplier of reasons for keeping people in their place has always been religion. We saw it at work in the debate over slavery. The Bible and the Qur'an both took slavery for granted. They took the subordination of women for granted too. So we run up against the awkward fact that sacred texts can be used to supply ammunition for those who want to keep people under control.

And they can still be used in that way today. For fundamentalist Christians the emancipation of women from male control is a colossal problem, because the Bible says women should be subordinate to men and never have authority over them. To this day most of Christianity still refuses to allow women to enter the official ministry of the Church. The subject is not even up for discussion in the Catholic Church, by far the largest organisation on the planet, with more than a billion members. Even the more liberal versions of Christianity struggled with it for ages. It was only in 2015 that the Church of England allowed women to be made bishops. Just as they learned to adapt to Darwin, liberal religions are learning to adapt, however painfully, to the liberation of women. But time does not stand still and they now have to deal, even more painfully, with the emancipation of gay people.

All this is hard enough for Christianity. For a number of reasons it is even harder for Islam. And here the struggle to come to terms with change has become violent. Fundamentalist Muslims are not only angry; in their most extreme form they have become brutally homicidal. There are many factors that contribute to this crisis in Islam, many of them outside the scope of this book. But they share a common problem with religious fundamentalists everywhere, including those in Israel. There are fundamentalist Jews in Israel who reject any attempt to share the Holy Land with Palestinians. They argue that God gave Palestine to them thousands of years ago and they are only taking back what was stolen from them. If you try to point out the dangers in that position they repeat what Christian fundamentalists said to Darwin. We are right and you are wrong because the Bible tells us so.

Since it is the Bible or the Qur'an that is used in this way, it seems that they are the problem, the reason these conflicts erupt. Or, to put it another way: it is the idea that these texts are revelations from God that is the difficulty. After all, I can argue with you about the status of women or gay people and we can agree or disagree. But when you tell me that your angle on these subjects is not yours but God's, then argument becomes impossible. It becomes a rerun of the Monkey Trial.

Fundamentalists don't debate. They don't try the evidence. They deliver a sentence. And it's always 'guilty' because their holy book has already decided the issue. This means that the crisis of fundamentalism in our time, including its violent versions, poses a question that goes to the heart of religions that claim to be based on a revelation that came directly from God. Surely, if it is used to justify not only the love of ignorance but the love of violence then there is something fundamentally wrong with it, to borrow their own language. So how can religion get itself off this particular hook? That's the question we'll consider in the next chapter when we look more closely at religion's violent history.

CHAPTER 39

Holy Wars

Is religion the main cause of violence in human history, as many have suggested? Religion is certainly no stranger to violence. It has used it in the past and it uses it today. But is it the *cause* of violence? Many thoughtful people think it is. And they go on to suggest that the way to rid the world of violence is to rid it of religion. Some push the argument further by saying that since it was God who commanded the violence that has been such a curse to humanity, the best way to save humanity from its curse is to get rid of God. It's a powerful charge and one we can't ignore.

If we confine the discussion to the three Abrahamic religions, Judaism, Christianity and Islam, the charge seems to stick. There's a lot of violence in the early history of Judaism. The liberation of the Jews from slavery in Egypt could not have been achieved without it; which is why we should pause here to ask whether the violence was necessary. Few people have ever claimed that violence against others is never justified. It is always an evil, but sometimes it is the lesser of two evils. Slavery was an evil. It treated men and women not as humans but as animals who could be disposed of at the whim of their masters. Most people today would support the right of slaves to rise against their owners and fight for their freedom. That's what the Jews did. They rose against their masters and escaped into the desert. What happened next is where it gets difficult.

Around 1300 BCE the Israelites did to the tribes who lived in Canaan (now Palestine) – tribes they believed were sinners against God – what Christian settlers did to Native Americans in the nineteenth century. The modern word we use to describe the uprooting and destruction of a whole people is *genocide*. It fits the bill here. And it's the Bible on which the charge must be pinned. Historians may argue about how long the settlement of the Jews in Palestinian lands actually took and how violent it actually was. The Bible is clear about the killing that occurred. And it says God ordered it. The book that describes it is called Joshua. It's a text sprinkled with phrases such as 'thou shalt utterly destroy them' and 'they destroyed them' and 'they did not leave any that breathed'. Joshua tells us the settlement of the tribes of Israel in the Promised Land was achieved through acts of violence commanded by God.

When we come to Christianity the record shows that it too had a violent beginning. But it was the object, not the subject, of the violence. In its early years it did not expect to be around long enough to get involved in worldly politics. Not that that stopped it being persecuted. It worshipped a crucified God and embraced its own suffering. That came to an end when the Emperor Constantine adopted it and put it to work on his behalf. After that the Church developed a taste for violence and learned how to use it as an instrument of control. For centuries it used violence against Jews, calling them 'God slayers' because of the crucifixion of Jesus, forgetting everything he had said in the Sermon on the Mount in the process. During the Crusades it used violence against Muslims. During the Inquisition it used violence against heretical Christians. And in the religious wars that followed the Reformation rival Christian groups fought against each other until society tired of their violence and stepped in to stop it.

Islam also had a violent birth. Though the idea of *jihad* or struggle can be understood in non-violent ways, it has also been

used to justify violence against infidels or unbelievers. Like
Christians, Muslims have been active in killing fellow believers
who followed a different version of the faith. Shias and Sunnis have
slaughtered each other as eagerly as Protestants and Catholics ever
did in Christianity. And the hatred between them is one of the
main causes of conflict in the Middle East today.

So the question is not whether religion has been the cause of
much of the violence in history, but why it should bother us? In our
glance at slavery, we noted that there are situations in which
violence is a valid moral option. That is a principle that guides
most nations in their internal as well as their external politics.
Statistically, the USA is the most Christian nation on earth. It is
also one of the most violent. It permits capital punishment. It
believes in the right of ordinary citizens to own firearms and use
them in self-defence. And thousands of its citizens are killed every
year as a consequence. It has also, like nations everywhere, used
violence not only to defend itself against its enemies but to intervene in the affairs of other countries. If we can justify violence in
these circumstances, why do we get so upset when religions use it
to serve their purposes? We are a violent species. So why does religious violence make us so squeamish?

There are two reasons. The first is that when religion enters a
quarrel it adds a toxic ingredient to the mix that is not always
present in other conflicts. Humans are prone to violence anyway,
but if they can persuade themselves they are doing it in obedience
to God it removes any chance of mercy and moderation from the
conflict. During a period of religious warfare in Scotland in the
seventeenth century known as 'the Killing Times', the battle cry of
one side was 'God and no quarter', meaning that they should show
no mercy and take no prisoners. Watching rival Muslim factions
shelling each other in the Middle East on this evening's TV News
we are likely to hear them praising Allah as they release their
missiles against each other.

If you are acting in obedience to the moral judge of the universe
you can't go wrong. 'God and no quarter!' That's why conflicts
between religious fanatics can roll through the centuries with

neither side ever seeking reconciliation. And when an old feud acquires a new surge of energy it is sometimes described as 'identity politics'. An unpopular group can achieve a sense of purpose and identity by wielding a faith that defines it against others. It can relieve an outsider's feelings of homelessness. It can intoxicate him with anger. And it can give him a reason for blowing himself up in an overcrowded Underground train in London in 2005.

If the first reason religious violence appals us is the unreasoning intensity it brings to human conflict, the second is that there is a terrible contradiction at its heart. It is a contradiction that unbelievers often see more clearly than believers. The name of the contradiction is God. Most religions are based on the claim that God is the supreme reality. And that he is the author of their moral code. They may have different ways of putting it, but they all see God as the universal parent. Humans are God's children. As the New Testament says, in God 'we live and move and have our being'.

But if we are all God's children, why does God spend so much time in history ordering one branch of his universal family to wipe out another branch? Why did his love for his Jewish children have to be expressed by the extermination of his Palestinian children? Why did he later abandon his Jewish children in favour of his Christian children and encourage his new favourites to torment their older siblings? Why did he order his Muslim children who worship him as One to persecute his pagan children who worship him as Many? Why is there so much violence in religious history, all done by groups who claim God is on their side?

Unless you are prepared to believe that God actually plays favourites like some kind of demented tyrant, then there are only two ways out of this dilemma. The obvious one is to decide that there is no God. What is called God is a human invention used, among other things, to justify humankind's love of violence and hatred of strangers. Getting rid of God won't solve the problem of human violence but it will remove one of its pretexts.

But if you don't want to abandon God then you have to do some hard thinking. You have to ask yourself what is more likely: that God is the kind of homicidal maniac religion often makes him out to be? Or that religion has got God wrong and confuses its own cruelty with his will? If you decide it is more likely that religion has misunderstood God than that God is the monster its preachers sometimes make him out to be then you have a problem.

It turns out that religion may be a greater enemy of God than atheism. Atheism says God doesn't exist. If God does exist he is more likely to be amused than outraged by the atheist's impudence. The atheist will learn soon enough! But if God is not a monster then he is unlikely to be amused by religious teachers who make him out to be one. So we arrive at the conclusion that though religion claims to reveal the true nature of God to the world, a lot of the time it is actually hiding God behind the thick fog of its own cruelty.

We catch occasional glimpses in scripture of the idea that religion is God's fiercest opponent. We find it stated in the words of Jesus who noticed how easy it was to use religion not only as a reason for doing evil things but as an excuse for not doing good things. It was bad religion that prompted the priest and his assistant to pass by on the other side because the man who had fallen among thieves *was not one of them!*

So yes, religion has caused and continues to cause some of the worst violence in history. And yes, it has used God to justify it. So if we mean by God the loving creator of the universe, then either he doesn't exist or religion has got him wrong. Either way, religion should make us wary. That doesn't necessarily mean we should abandon it altogether. We may decide to stick with it but to do so with humility, admitting the evil it has done as well as the good. It's up to us.

But there were some who were so appalled by religion's bloodthirsty record that they were determined to tame it and put it in its place. In our last chapter we'll look at how they did it.

CHAPTER 40

The End of Religion?

My dog hates it when the first week of November comes round. In the gardens and parks near where I live people explode fireworks far into the night. The noise will cause Daisy to quiver in fear. To hide from the enemy who's after her she will try to dig a hole in the carpet of my study. She is in no danger, but I can't get her to understand that. She has what is known as a *hyperactive agency detection device* or HADD. She is detecting a threat that doesn't exist. This can happen to any of us. A floor creaks in the attic and we imagine an intruder. Then the rational part of us kicks in and we realise that a sudden gust of wind caused the old floor to shiver. Daisy can't reason like that, which is why early November and its gunpowder season is a nightmare for her. She is programmed to respond to loud noises by running away, and no explanation from me can get her to understand that no one is hunting her.

Daisy is not the only creature in history to have developed HADD. It influenced most of humanity for centuries. Religion had told men and women that the world was controlled not by natural laws but by supernatural forces. The word for this is *superstition*, the belief that things can happen by magic without any natural cause. That way of thinking began to change in the seventeenth century during a period that became known as the Enlightenment, when science replaced superstition as the best way to explain what went on in the world. Everything had a natural cause. There was a reason for everything that happened. The motto of the Enlightenment was 'Dare to Know'. Don't give in to superstition. Dare to know the true cause of things. One of the consequences of the Enlightenment was to loosen the hold supernatural explanations had on the human mind. Lights went on in people's heads and they started thinking for themselves.

If daring to know how nature worked was one of the impulses of the Enlightenment, another was disgust with centuries of religious violence. Superstition was bad enough. War was worse. The thinkers of the Enlightenment noticed how religions always disagreed with each other. Each believed it possessed the truth revealed by God and the others were wrong. And when it got control of a country it tried to make everyone march to its drumbeat. That was bad enough. It was worse if there were just two religions in a country competing against each other. They would be at each other's throats all the time, as they had been in Europe since the Reformation. But if there were thirty religions they all seemed to live in peace!

The Enlightenment drew two conclusions from this. The first was that the more religions there were in a society the safer it would be for everyone. So the best guarantee of peace was to outlaw discrimination and practise toleration. Their second conclusion was that, while religion should be tolerated *within* society, it should never be given control *over* society. The authority of religious leaders should be confined to their own faith communities.

It was only in the USA that this principle was ever strictly enforced. The authors of the American Constitution had been influenced by Enlightenment thinking on religion. They remembered how America's first settlers had fled religious persecution in Europe. And they were determined to avoid it in their new promised land. That's why Thomas Jefferson, one of the authors of the Declaration of Independence and third president of the young republic, advised the American people to 'make no law respecting an establishment of religion or prohibiting the free exercise thereof'. They should build a wall of separation between Church and State. And that became one of the founding principles of the USA.

Things were more complicated in Europe where Church and State had been entangled for centuries. But the ideas unleashed by the Enlightenment started to undermine the authority of religion in the affairs of the State. In time a more radical split between Church and State was achieved in Europe than in the USA where religion, though it has no official position, still has considerable social and political influence.

What happened in Europe was the emergence of what is now called the *secular state*. The word secular comes from the Latin *saeculum* meaning a period of time. It came to mean time as against eternity, the world in contrast to the Church, human thinking as opposed to religious revelation. The secular state chose not to interfere with those who ran their lives on principles derived from religion. But it decided to base its own decisions only on principles derived from this world. Here are a couple of examples of how this works today.

As we've seen, many religions discriminate against women. Their sacred books tell them God destined women to be helpers to men and never to have authority over them. In secular societies to discriminate against women is held to be morally wrong and in some cases it has been made a crime that can land you in court. Nevertheless, given the secular principle that lets religion do its own thing within its own community, the state often turns a blind eye to practices in faith communities that would be a crime in society.

The other example concerns homosexuality. Again, religion's sacred books disapprove. Gay sex is always a sin and one for which you can be executed. In some parts of the world it can still get you killed today. But in most modern secular societies the persecution of gay people is itself a crime. Homosexuals are now afforded the same rights as heterosexuals, including, in many countries, the right to marry. Yet the secular state turns a blind eye to the discrimination against gay people that is practised in many faith communities.

While the secular *state* may ignore the sexism and homophobia of faith communities, many of its *citizens* pay them a lot of attention and don't like what they see. Because, as well as the emergence of the secular *state*, the Enlightenment gave birth to the secular *mind*, a way of thinking about life that makes no reference to God and his views on how the world should be ordered. The secular mind does more than reject the application of religious principles to its own life. It is appalled by the effect religion can have on the lives of others. It opposes those who discriminate against women and gay people on the basis of holy writings from the Late Bronze Age. The emergence of the secular mind has resulted in the gradual erosion of the authority of religion in the West. And as a result, Christianity, the faith that dominated Europe for centuries, has begun a decline that shows little sign of stopping.

It is a decline that saddens many people, including some who have ceased to practise religion themselves. They know that the Church developed many vices in its long voyage through history, but they also acknowledge that it had its virtues as well. It has been a friend as well as an enemy of humanity, a healer as well as a tormentor. But human nature hates a vacuum. So the gap left by the fading of Christianity in the West has prompted the formation of a movement called *secular humanism*. It doesn't qualify for definition as a religion, but since it has borrowed some of religion's best ideas a quick look at it will be a good way to end this history.

As their name suggests, secular humanists try to help men and women live good lives, not on principles imposed by religion but on principles humans have worked out for themselves. They believe humanity has grown up and should now take responsibility for itself. In its childhood it was told by religion, or God, what to do and what not to do. And some of the instructions were shocking. Slavery, the oppression of women, the stoning of gay people, forced conversion and punishment for believing the wrong things? They could do a better job than that! Being human themselves, they were in the best position to know what was good for humanity. Tolerance was good. Persecution was bad. Kindness was good. Cruelty was bad. You didn't have to believe in God to see that. You didn't need religion to tell you that loving your neighbours and treating them as you yourself would like to be treated made sense.

Secular humanists were happy to work with any group that wanted to make the world a better place, including faith groups. They were even prepared to steal some of religion's clothes. Humanists were aware that good things were being lost with the decline of religion, so they did their best to recover some of them and use them in a humanistic way. Religion was good at helping people mark the big turning points in their lives. Being born. Getting married. Dying. Religion had ceremonies for these occasions. The trouble was that they involved the heavenly world secular humanists didn't believe in. Babies had to be cleansed of sin. Couples were told marriage was for life whether they liked it or not. And the dead were all going on to another life. Humanists didn't believe any of that.

So they started writing their own services. And the modern secular state licensed them to perform them. Humanist celebrants now conduct as many weddings in Scotland as Christian ministers. They lead funerals. They conduct naming ceremonies for babies. They have become good at tailoring these ceremonies to the particular needs of the people who have requested them. A humanist celebrant can help them put their own values and preferences into the event. And in so doing give them personal significance. They can impart a different kind of spirituality to moments in life that were once monopolised by traditional religion. Secular spirituality finds meaning and beauty in *this* life. It is the only life we'll ever have, so we should be grateful for it and use it well.

This is not the only thing secular humanists borrow from religion. They admire the way people of faith come together for worship and the experience of being with each other. They mix with and offer support to people they might otherwise never meet. Weekly attendance at worship is an opportunity to be serious and examine the kind of life you are leading. And maybe decide to make some changes. Secular humanists see the value of this. So they have created Sunday assemblies of their own. Sometimes this is known as 'church-going for atheists'. They meet for reflection and celebration. They listen to secular sermons and addresses. They sing songs. They keep moments of silence and reflection. It's religion without the supernatural: *human* religion.

It's too early to predict whether humanism of this sort will survive and grow or fade and die. Attempts at secular religion have been tried before and disappeared after a short run. Critics always say they're like drinking non-alcoholic beer or decaffeinated coffee. What's the point?

What all this proves is both the attraction and the difficulty of religion for secular-minded men and women. They may admire much of what religion has achieved, but they can no longer accept the supernatural beliefs on which it is based. They are suspicious of forms of authority that claim to be above human correction. They have noticed how slow religion is at adapting to good changes in human behaviour, as well as in accepting the consequences of new knowledge. Far from daring to know the new, religion usually prefers to cling to the old.

As we have already observed, religion is an anvil that has worn out many hammers. It may outlive secular humanism. Though it is in decline in many places today, it is still the biggest show on earth, and it's running at a place of worship near you. But it's entirely up to you whether you buy a ticket.

Index

'ill make you writhe, ripple
and froth with pleasure.'
—*Stephen Fry*

'Brilliant, irresistible: a
wonderful surprise.'
—*Philip Pullman*

Explore the LITTLE HISTORIES

Illuminating, energetic and readable, the Little Histories are books
that explore timeless questions and take readers young and old on an
enlightening journey through knowledge. Following in the footsteps of
E. H. Gombrich's irresistible tour de force *A Little History of the World*,
the family of Little Histories, sumptuously designed with unique
illustrations, is an essential library of human endeavour.

Which Little History will you read next?

A Little History of the World by E. H. Gombrich
A Little Book of Language by David Crystal
A Little History of Philosophy by Nigel Warburton
A Little History of Science by William Bynum
A Little History of Literature by John Sutherland
A Little History of the United States by James West Davidson
A Little History of Religion by Richard Holloway
A Little History of Economics by Niall Kishtainy

New titles coming soon!

For more information visit www.littlehistory.org

'Will make you writhe, ripple
and froth with pleasure.'
Stephen Fry

'Brilliant, irresistible: a
wonderful surprise.'
Philip Pullman

Explore the LITTLE HISTORIES

Illuminating, energetic and readable, the Little Histories are books
that explore timeless questions and take readers young and old on an
enlightening journey through knowledge. Following in the footsteps of
E. H. Gombrich's tour de force *A Little History of the World*, the family
of Little Histories, sumptuously designed with unique illustrations, is an
essential library of human endeavour.

Which Little History will you read next?

A Little History of the World by E. H. Gombrich
A Little Book of Language by David Crystal
A Little History of Philosophy by Nigel Warburton
A Little History of Science by William Bynum
A Little History of Literature by John Sutherland
A Little History of the United States by James West Davidson
A Little History of Religion by Richard Holloway
A Little History of Economics by Niall Kishtainy
A Little History of Archaeology by Brian Fagan

New titles coming soon!

For more about our books...

Visit our websites:

US – yalebooks.com

UK/Europe – yalebooks.co.uk

Or find us online:

🐦 twitter.com/littlehistoryof

f facebook.com/littlehistory

ⓗ littlehistory.org